Endorsements for
SPIRITUALLY HOMELESS

Kris Girrell has written a profoundly timely and necessary book. *Spiritually Homeless* speaks to the quiet ache many of us carry—a sense that something sacred exists beyond ourselves, but an uncertainty about how to name or engage with it. This is especially true for those raised in a specific faith tradition who now find themselves questioning, drifting, or searching.

With deep compassion and quiet wisdom, Kris shares his own journey and invites us to walk alongside him as fellow seekers. His reflections are tender, insightful, and refreshingly honest, offering a space of belonging for those navigating the often lonely terrain of spiritual exploration.

This book is a gift for anyone who has had the courage to ask where they truly belong when it comes to faith—and who longs to do so without shame, dogma, or fear. It is a gentle companion for the spiritually homeless, and a much-needed voice in today's fractured world.

Rebecca Williams, Executive Coach,
Spiritual Guide and former Chief Client Officer, Marietta, GA

"Right from the start, I was able to just dive in and take my on own journey - and this journey had several stops along the way that drew my attention into my own spiritual goo! Important stops - not because a particular piece of the content felt brand new or hard to grasp, but more because I was ready to hear it beyond the cognitive level. There is so much here!!!

The author allowed for that time beautifully by the journaling exercises and the strong encouragement to bring to a therapist what belongs inside that unique working relationship. For this reason, I think this book would be a great read as a group facilitated by a leader with a history of integrity moving in and out of psycho-spiritual leadership. The readers of this book are likely to have felt alone - or at least marginalized - by religious institutions; so the sound of other voices, within the book and in discussion groups would be affirming and enable an even deeper dive into the content.

It is possible some readers will recognize themselves here that have not been able to recognize, let alone name, name their spiritual existence before. What a gift to find a part of our name AND all the supporting and affirming history and research at the same time!"

Kathy Welch, retired Music Educator
and Spiritual Director, Asheland, North Carolins

Have you ever wondered about you and your relationship to your spirituality? Not as a passive spectator on this path but rather as an actively engaged participant in the journey'? For me, after countless years of internal discussions, after many deep reflections, after finding expression through journaling, and joining countless communities committed to this 'inquisition' --I have (finally!) found a book that provides access to my 'question'.

The book is *Spiritually Homeless: Finding Our Way Beyond Religion* by Kris Girrell.

Inside the pages of this text, the author is ready, willing, and (incredibly) able to engage each of us in an open, reasoned, and sincere dialogue, about the journey of finding our own spiritual discovery and destination.

With the journey through each chapter, I experienced a deep sensitivity toward the profoundly significant principles and practices that helped me achieve a deeper relationship to myself and my spirituality--guiding me to a deeper understanding of 'being--belonging–becoming' me!

Girrell provides many illustrations of his own personal story and journey, multiple stories from others on the journey, as well as a series of questions that help readers with their own inner discussion greatly. This is an intimate and informative book that readers on the path to spiritual discovery will find is purpose-driven for them as well.

The 'truth' (as subjectively as I can describe it as 'My Truth') is that *Spiritually Homeless: Finding Your Way Beyond Religion* is an important experience on multiple levels as it supports the reader to travel toward their 'path of purpose and partnership with the Divine' --I highly recommend it!"

Joseph Miglio, PhD, Associate Dean,
Berkeley School of Music, Lynnfield, MA

For those who feel alone in a religious crowd—for boundary crossers and holy misfits, for those who honor their questions as much as their faith—this book is a guide. Girrell writes with passion and experience, offering companionship to those seeking authentic spirituality beyond the bounds of inherited beliefs. With a wide range of personal stories from a broad range of spiritual seekers, with accessible wisdom and practical exercises, Spiritually Homeless invites readers to trust their spiritual intuition and discover what it means to be both truly spiritual and true to oneself. If you seek a meaningful spiritual life—one rooted in wonder rather than certainty—this book is for you.

Rev. Michael Reed, Executive Director MassIPL, Andover, MA

I loved this book, *Spiritually Homeless.* I wish that I had access to a book of this nature years ago, when I first began my own spiritual journey and felt so lost as to what was going on. I was leaving behind traditional conservative ideas about God, and did not know where to find support for the journey

I was on. My journey had evolved from fundamental Christianity and the dogma that it teaches, to seeking a "how to" guide in finding God, feeling God, knowing God, outside of just knowing scriptures. Girrell's book maps out his journey and how Girrell finds his way back to Source. It is clear that Kris has been around the block a few times on this spiritual quest and his experiences through it all ultimately landed him in the place he was seeking. Before I read *Spiritually Homeless,* I just groped along in the dark.

Spiritually Homeless lays out what it is like for us seekers who have left traditional ways of thinking and believing in God and guides us in seeing that there is a way through the maze, and we are not alone. I love how Kris maps out his own spiritual crises, including the dark night of the soul, and lets readers know that they are all part of the journey. I love how the author names what Spirit has looked like for him in his life, including his own personal experiences and the experiences of others on the journey. And I especially loved learning where we spiritually homeless might go now, for comfort, for connection with Source, and for community. Where is our home now? It feels obvious to me that Kris has forged his own journey into the mystery, and encourages us to follow along in finally finding our "tribe." I would recommend this book to any serious seeker of The Unknown Mystery. Thank you, Kris!

Mary Lynne Kemp, MD, Savannah, GA

Have you ever felt disconnected from your church, confused by rigid doctrine, or simply alone on your spiritual path? *Spiritually Homeless* by Kris Girrell is a deeply compassionate and wise guide for anyone who has ever found themselves in that wilderness—questioning, searching, and longing for something more meaningful.

Drawing on his own experience, years of research, and powerful interviews with others who've walked similar paths, Girrell offers both validation and direction. He doesn't prescribe a one-size-fits-all answer; instead, he invites readers into a thoughtful exploration of what it means to move from inherited belief systems to an authentic, personal spirituality.

This book is not just for those who have left organized religion—it's for anyone who has ever paused to ask, *Is there more to this than I've been told?* Girrell skillfully maps the terrain of the spiritual seeker's journey with clarity, depth, and heart. Whether you're deconstructing, rebuilding, or simply curious, *Spiritually Homeless* reminds you that you are not alone—and that the journey itself can be sacred.

Highly recommended for spiritual seekers, religious questioners, and anyone hungry for a deeper, more personal connection with the divine.

Linda Manning, Transformational Coach and Consultant, Concord MA

SPIRITUALLY HOMELESS

Finding Our Way Beyond Religion

KRIS GIRRELL

For information, contact
MSI Press, LLC
1760-F Airline Hwy #203
Hollister, CA 95023

Copyeditors: Dr. Geri Henderson, Dr. Betty Lou Leaver
Cover design & layout: Opeyemi Ikuborije
ISBN: 978-1-957354-77-4
Library of Congress Control Number: 2025910972

Permission for reprinted materials granted by:

David Whyte and Many Rivers Company: "The Opening of Eyes" and "The Well of Grief" Mirabai Starr. *Saint John of the Cross: Devotions, prayers & living wisdom*

Mirabai Starr: *Unknowing*, a translation from *Saint John of the Cross: Devotions, prayers & living wisdom*. Sounds True, 2008 (by personal communication)

Bernadette Noll, *I Want to Age Like Sea Glass*. By personal communication.

"Out beyond the ideas of wrongdoing and rightdoing, there is a field. I'll meet you there. When the soul lies down in that grass, the world is too full to talk about. Ideas, language, even the phrase 'each other' doesn't make any sense."

- Jelaluddin Rumi (1207-1273)

CONTENTS

PART ONE:
WHERE DO WE START?

CHAPTER ONE

At the end of the day, your feet should be dirty,
your hair messy and your eyes sparkling.

Shanti

If we go back far enough all of us have ancestors who looked up at
the stars and asked questions.

Brian Swimme

Everyday Spirituality

Have you ever gotten lost in a flower blossom? Have you ever welled up with tears looking into a newborn's eyes? And when you last walked barefoot through the green grass, didn't you feel the earth reaching up to tickle your feet as she greeted your every step? While they might not sound like it, these are just some of the many ways we can experience spirituality every day.

I would wager that everyone has had a spiritual experience. That may sound to you like hyperbole, but I assure you that I say it with a high degree of certainty. It's just that the term spirituality has so often been conflated with something religious that many may have had a quite spiritual experience but because it was seen as "non-religious" it was dismissed or overlooked. Spirituality is a human experience; it's something we all have. Your experience, however, is different and unique—probably different in every way from mine or your sibling's or best friend's, but it is spiritual, nonetheless. Just because you have never shared it in ritual or in any formal setting does not lessen the nature or the impact that spiritual experience has had on you. As French philosopher and theologian, Teilhard de Chardin is often quoted as saying, "we are spiritual beings having a human experience.[1]" Likewise, Bill Wilson, the author of the *Big Book of Alcoholics Anonymous* (Alcoholics Anonymous, 1976), wrote an entire chapter to the agnostics where he talked about everyday moments that could be felt as spiritual, like staring at the beauty of a sunset or seeing a newborn baby.

In a way, *Spiritually Homeless* is about those experiences, how and where we find and experience them and how we might be able to find others whose spirituality has been found outside any religious institution or instruction. It is about how we can find our people, our community, and find our home as spiritual but not religious (SBNR) people. That phrase is one that is heard more and more in the world of religion, and for many within organized religion it sounds like a rejection of standards and commitments. It's as if the organized "Church" hears those words as saying, "I belong to no one and no accountability system; I'm just me." Others may label the SBNR as perhaps just a postmodern expression of individualism. But we who genuinely claim that status, SBNR, know ours to be a difficult and often lonely path. What is different for many of us is that we have had multiple experiences that we feel are truly spiritual and sacred and which neither match what the organized religions have described nor even fit into their practiced narrative. These not-so-ordinary moments in our ordinary lives point us toward our spiritual nature. Sometimes these moments have us catch our breath, and sometimes they can stop us dead in our tracks like the following personal experience.

---

1. This quote is often attributed to Pierre Teilhard de Chardin in *The Joy of Kindness* (1993), by Robert J. Furey, p. 138; but it is attributed to G. I. Gurdjieff in *Beyond Prophecies and Predictions: Everyone's Guide To the Coming Changes* (1993) by Moira Timms, p. 62; however, neither cite a source. It was mostly popularized by Wayne Dyer, who often quotes it in his presentations, crediting it to Chardin, as does Stephen Covey in *Living the 7 Habits: Stories of Courage and Inspiration* (2000), p. 47

In my early and mid-adult years, I was an avid back country hiker. I loved the mountains and the forests with their pristine, gurgling streams and comforting beds of deep moss on which I would sleep. But what I enjoyed most of all was the point where I became just a living being—not human, not animal—just an organism breathing and moving through space. The first time I felt this was breaking above tree line in the mountains. While in the woods, the trees and rocks reflected the sound of my footsteps and breathing. I could hear the squirrels rustling in the leaves and the birds flitting about from branch to branch. In the distance, I would catch the sounds of a hidden waterfall, and the awareness I had is that of being one of the many elements— rocks, streams, trees and humans—in this environment.

But then comes that moment where the scrub pines and stunted vegetation gives way to nothing but rock and lichen. There is nothing to reflect the sound of my breath. There is perhaps a sound that the breeze makes as it passes my ear. But the stunning awareness was that I was not capable of hearing myself. No breathing, no footsteps, no aural evidence of my passing through. I had read Douglass Harding's book, *On Having No Head,* and had done some of his exercises in conscious awareness, but I had never experienced it like that moment. I could see my legs and my boots as they moved from rock to rock. But I could not find any awareness of my head, my consciousness, my breathing, or my separateness as a being. When the sound of my breathing disappeared, my head and my beingness went with it! There was no longer a "me" or a "my" that was separate and distinct from the rest of everything. I was one with it, as it was one with all of whatever I was experiencing.

I refer to that moment as a "spiritual experience" when telling others about it. But I don't really know what it was. I was filled and empty at the same time. I was nothing and yet everything else. There was no boundary between me and it. Objectivity had vanished. I sat down on a large rock facing the black, white, and gray vista of the Rockies, but I was not conscious of my butt on the rock nor of the distance between me and that vista. I was just in it and a part of it, almost as if I were a mountain or a rock or maybe the air itself. As that filled me, I began to well up with tears and cry—not from any sadness or joy, but from the fullness which seemed to be leaking out of my eyes.

Nothing in the Bible had prepared me for that moment—and nothing I had ever learned in school, seminary, or the church of my childhood. But I was clear that it was a transcendent spiritual experience. Those of us on this path of spirituality have other—similar or not at all similar—experiences that teach us about our spiritual nature. Each of those is as personal and unique as my mountaintop headless experience. Yours is most likely different, and yet I would wager that you know what I am talking about. David Deida (2005) in his book, *Finding God Through Sex*, talks about making love as a spiritually transcendent experience, where two in fact do become one. Transcendent experiences range as wide and far as hiking in the woods, to making love, to sitting in a cathedral. In having such personal encounters, you most likely had no one or nowhere to turn to help you unpack and understand what just happened.

Spirituality is a basic and fundamental element of our meaning-making. The nature of our brains is that they are designed to create meaning: "this means that." Brains do that so that we have a sense of understanding and order in our otherwise chaotic world. From the time of our birth (and perhaps even for months before then), our brains are busy making some sense of everything we sense or perceive. My wife runs an early childhood education center, and I love going there to watch the infants. You can actually see them discovering that their hand is attached and a part of them and then see them light up when they discover that this hand thing can touch something that they see. From that time on, we are busily making meaning out of our experiences. So, when it comes to our spirituality, codifying certain experiences as "spiritual" and meaningful is a core process. We seem to place greater meaning on some experiences and feelings than others. We extrapolate from those core experiences to making such interpretations as "I am divine" or "you and I share the divine spark of life" and "this thing or experience is sacred." Spirituality is a part of the meaning-making process.

Spirituality is also unique and individual, but denominations and religions are general. They talk of the great mystics' experiences as if those are what we should aspire to have but probably wouldn't since we are mere mortals. Religions and their leaders, by their very function, must speak to the masses in generalized terms and not in the specifics of your spiritual experience or mine. The result is a kind of disconnect between us with our unique specific experiences and the generalities of traditional religion, between us and other forms of travel along the spiritual paths, between us and what we are supposed to believe the nature of the Divine encounter is. There is no way the generalities of religion fit our personal and unique spirituality. For many, it feels as though we have outgrown our religion. We just no longer fit in. This is what it feels like to be spiritually homeless.

Welcome.

Spiritual homelessness is a feeling that many of us have experienced at one time or another in our lives. It's that feeling of being adrift, of not quite fitting in, of not being able to find a spiritual home that resonates with us on a deep level. It is a feeling that can be incredibly isolating and disheartening. The ways of the organized religions, the tenets of their doctrines, and even the prayers and rituals which we used to find so reassuring, no longer do it for us. We feel as though we have entered a wilderness, a desert that holds no water or nourishment for our souls. As a result, we feel dry and hungry—not so much in the literal meaning of water and food but in the spiritual sense. We read the passage in Matthew, "Blessed are those who hunger and thirst," and yet it doesn't feel "blessed" in the least.

Much like the other elements of the blessings Jesus spoke of in perhaps his first attempt at public preaching, the thought that we would become satisfied when we are in fact hungry and thirsty for anything sounds at the very least to be counter-intuitive and, at the worst, out of our range of understanding. Spiritual homelessness feels a bit like a wilderness, and this seemingly inhospitable wilderness beckons like the sirens calling the Argonauts or the Lorelei that called to the riverboats on the Rhine. It is a hunger that seems insatiable, but it only appears that way because we are trapped within our very human logic of meritocracy and dualistic cause-and-effect. In this wilderness, and in our homelessness, there is no cause and effect; there is no deserving or entitlement. There is just sensation and awareness, and an awareness of something pulling us forward.

Relax.

Exhale.

You are not alone exploring and trying to find your way in this wilderness. There are others like you (and me). In fact, what if I told you that feeling homeless spiritually isn't necessarily a bad thing? What if I told you that it's actually a sign of spiritual growth and evolution? What if I told you that which you already sense, that you are on a path to a deeper and more intimate understanding of the Divine, one which an increasing number of humans claim as their form of spirituality?

As perhaps you do. And as I do as well.

This book is about that journey, not just the unique experiences we have. As individually unique as each of our paths can be—that's one of the earmarks of this journey, there are some common threads we can discuss. We will explore those commonalities as well as help you to describe your own uniqueness. We will dig deeply into the dynamics that shape our path, why we may have left organized religion or had never seen it as viable in the first place. We will explore how spiritual experiences transform us and pull us forward. There are others who have gone before us and many others who will eventually venture into this same wilderness. Though it is not a simple quest, we pack our bags with all we need for the journey, rest when we are tired, cry when we are moved to, sit in contemplation of the awe and wonder of it all, and rejoice at every new discovery.

Being spiritually homeless is a mystical journey—the path of the mystics. Mystics are those whose experience of the Divine is personal. Mystics trust their experience over the teachings of the various religions and even in preference over the words of the sages. Mystics often make up their own terminology and language about their experiences of the Divine if only because the traditional words carry with them the background and context of the traditional religion, and, often, they want to distance themselves from those traditional thoughts and paradigms. At the same time, mystics are not at all embarrassed or ashamed of their experience and humbly offer their insights to anyone who will listen. If you are on this journey, you are a mystic. You may not be understood by anyone who is not also on this spiritual journey—it takes one to know one, as the saying goes! At the same time, you may not even have words to describe your experience. It is just a knowing.

And yet, we are still left without a home. We are left with a longing for community. We are, after all, social creatures, born to be in relationship with others. And while we can and often do worship, pray, meditate, sing, and even fall speechless at times, we feel mostly alone within those experiences. We still need and want some kind of home. Traditional houses of worship have failed us. They have not continued to grow and evolve. They remain fixed on the teaching of their various founders, and so we have moved on.

Within the pages of this book, we will explore the two poles of why we left and what pulls us forward. We will explore the many phases of spiritual development and evolution. We will look for trail blazes left by those who have gone through the wilderness before us, both the sages and some ordinary folk like you and me. And we will explore the varied ways we find or create meaning, the things that inspire us and the hope of finding a new home.

If you have picked up this book and read just these first few paragraphs and pages, you know what I mean. *Spiritually Homeless* is about your journey and written for you. But be comforted: I will not preach. I may, however, interpret scriptures in a new and perhaps novel way. But then, so do you. We are siblings. Fellow explorers. Innocents rubbing the dust from our eyes so that we can see more clearly. We are like the poet David Whyte (2012, p. 31) described in *The Opening of Eyes (reprinted below with permission from David Whyte and Many Rivers Press)*:

The Opening of Eyes

That day I saw beneath dark clouds
the passing light over the water
and I heard the voice of the world speak out,
I knew then, as I have before
life is no passing memory of what has been
nor the remaining pages of a great book
waiting to be read.

It is the opening of eyes long closed.
It is the vision of far off things
seen for the silence they hold.
It is the heart after years
of secret conversing
speaking out loud in the clear air.

It is Moses in the desert
fallen to his knees before the lit bush.
It is the man throwing away his shoes
as if to enter heaven
and finding himself astonished,
opened at last,
Fallen in love with solid ground.

Ever since I first read that poem, I have known that Whyte was one of us. There are many, many more who journey on this spiritual path, and we will draw from their wisdom. In the end, we will weave together the threads that define this journey. My intention is to keep chapters on the short side—thorough enough to convey the thought but succinct enough to be digestible. I will provide some ways to reinterpret how and why those seeking spirituality evolved to this place. Without trying to generalize too much, we will look into some of the more common routes into spiritual homelessness. I will ask questions that may not have answers or which disturb and disquiet you. Asking those types of thought-provoking questions should be the function of religion and was at some point in our past.

Please know that I have nothing against churches and religions, per se. It is just that many of us on this journey of faith find ourselves outside those structures and institutions. Churches can be beautiful and sacred places. In fact, some churches and cathedrals can precipitate a spiritual experience simply stepping inside. If you have ever set foot in Barcelona's Sagrada Familia Cathedral, you know what I mean. You are suddenly bathed in a rainbow of light, and because the ceiling is a series of parabolic dishes, whatever music is playing gets reflected down at you from many angles and seems to come from everywhere around you.

When I was in graduate school at Penn State, my internship was working in the Career Development Center under the guidance of Dr. Karl Bartsch. Besides being a psychologist, Karl was also a Mennonite minister from British Colombia. Mennonite houses of worship are plain buildings—nothing that would indicate that what you are looking at is a house of worship. Karl and I were fortunate to have written a paper that we were to present at the national conference of the American Psychological Association in New York City. While we were in New York, Karl wanted to go to see St. Patrick's Cathedral, so we made time to visit. The building was under renovation, replete with scaffolding and drop cloths around the back, but still open to the public. As

I was walking down the center aisle of the cathedral, I turned to look back at my mentor. Tears were running down his face as he looked in awe at the high vaulted ceiling. "I always wondered why they built these things," he whispered, barely able to speak. I didn't need to ask whether he thought this to be a spiritual experience—it was quite clear! Like David Whyte's Moses, Karl had fallen in love.

The Art and Craft of Exploring

Spiritual experiences are what move us, and more important, our spiritual experiences are what guide us onto this path. But how do you navigate this path? How do you find your way in a world that often seems hostile to spiritual exploration and growth? Given that I see this as a path of exploration, there will be markers along the way to help us out on the journey.

Caution Sign – Throughout this discussion, these will be placed where either I as an author or you as an explorer will find it necessary to exercise caution. One example is that I must be continually aware that as a large white male elder, I have a lens of privilege through which I have perceived much of the world. I must take caution not to generalize my perceptions to other groups or to you the reader.

Information – Some of the areas we will explore are subjects that go well beyond the scope of this text and may only need to be named here. In such cases, I will provide links to further information. Some will be cited references, and others might include QR codes that will take you directly to the deeper dive.

Rough Road Ahead – At times, we will encounter some difficult navigation. These are issues that are tough to deal with but nonetheless must be traveled. These are issues like death and dying, grief and pain-producing situations that are naturally occurring.

Winding Road Ahead – Many topics require a more detailed explanation that may at times feel like a long winding road. While I will try to keep this to a minimum, topics like aspects of the Dark Night of the Soul are complex and need a fuller explanation.

Danger – There are times when we can get way over our heads on this journey. We may seek advice from people who are within the very system from which we left, whether that be family or the religious sect we no longer fit. We may seek teachers or gurus who espouse another approach but want us to follow "the" one way they teach.

I may not fully identify each of the hazards on this journey but call these out in an effort to be as aware of the issues we face as I possibly can. Nonetheless, this is a journey, to be sure. It is not a place or a set of principles but rather an on-going process.

What You'll Need on the Journey

First and foremost, every journey starts at some fixed place and time. Only you can identify your exact place, but we will begin this exploration discussing how we got here and where exactly "t/here" is. Without knowing where we are starting from, finding direction and setting off toward our destination cannot be established.

Second, we need some guidance—a compass if you will. Our compass on this journey is composed of your values and the four ordinal directions, which are something like Experience, Accessibility, Heart/Love, and Community. But unlike the traditional compass that points to our North Star or Southern Cross (depending on your hemisphere), our ordinal directions are the litmus tests for the experiences we have along this journey. Is this a pure and relatable experience we can trust? Is it something that we and others can access or find on the journey? Does the experience relate to heart or love as its purest expression? And does it present an opening to creating community and belonging?

Third, we will need a map. In our case, we will be relying on the maps created by early and contemporary explorers of the journey, specifically those who have traveled through the dark night of the soul (the place of spiritual impasse). These descriptions may be extremely helpful when we find that there is no actual sense of direction or moral compass that works any longer. Tapping into the outline by John of the Cross—with some significant alteration to fit the postmodern experience—will at least give us labels for identifying what might be happening to us.

Finally, and this comes from the many experiences of hiking and backpacking in the wild, what will sustain us and nurture us on the journey? Do we have a source of food or nurturance? What are the books you take on your journey? What are your rituals that nourish you in your form of spirituality? Bottom line: what feeds you spiritually?

Let me end this chapter with a few tips:

- Be open to new experiences and ideas. Don't be afraid to explore different spiritual traditions and practices. You may find that certain practices or beliefs resonate with you more than others.

- Trust your own inner guidance. You have an innate sense of what is right for you, and you don't need anyone else to tell you what that is. Listen to your intuition, and trust that you will be guided to the right path.

- Seek out community. While you may not find a traditional spiritual home that fits with your beliefs and practices, you can still find like-minded individuals who are also on the path to spiritual growth. Seek out community events, online forums, and other opportunities to connect with others who share your values and goals.

- Keep a journal. Doing so will not only help you record and revisit your thoughts and musings about your spiritual explorations, it also will be like leaving breadcrumbs on the trail should you want to find your way back home. I believe it was Ben Franklin who once said, "live a life worth writing about," or something like that,

- Finally, spiritual homelessness is not a curse but a blessing in disguise. It is a sign that you are ready to take your spiritual journey to the next level and that you are willing to explore the vast and mysterious realm of the Divine on your own terms. So, embrace your spiritual homelessness, embrace your spiritual wandering, and know that you are on the path to a deeper and more meaningful spiritual experience.

Journaling: Take a moment to reflect on your spiritual journey. What have been the highs and lows of your journey so far? Draw a horizontal line across the middle of a page in your journal and, assuming that to be an emotional midpoint, plot your spiritual journey's highs (above the line) and lows (below it) across time from your early memories of spiritual beliefs and experiences to where you are now. Make a few notes on your chart about what was happening at each peak and valley. Then, journal on what the highs have in common and what the lows have in common.

CHAPTER TWO

I had no idea where I was, but when I found myself there (without knowing where there was) I suddenly understood sublime things, ineffable things. I will not even try to say what I felt as I let myself down into the arms of unknowing. This embrace transcends all thought.

St John of the Cross, *Devotions, Prayers & Living Wisdom*

How Did We Get Here?

It is a curious thing that the word *nowhere* could be divided into the two words *now here*. Being and becoming spiritually homeless is a lot like that. We feel that we are somehow nowhere, and yet we sense that we are grounded in the present, this moment, right here and right now. But it would serve us to first look at how we arrived at "now here."

From a historical and predominantly Christian perspective, this country (the United States of America) was not originally a religion-oriented population with estimates that only about 10% of the colonists belonged to some religion. Though some people came to the New Land to escape religious persecution and though those stories are the ones we most often hear, the bulk of the population was relatively non-affiliated with any type of religion or sect. However, over a century later, following the Revolutionary War, those numbers rose to about 17%. That stayed relatively the same as the population of the States grew, but following the Civil War, the percentages rose dramatically. Davis and Graham tapped into a number of sources and census data to report that, in the 25years "from 1870 to 1895, attendance at some house of worship more than doubled, from 13.5 million people to 32.7 million, as the general population grew from 38.6 million to 69.6 million people. The net result was a 12 percent increase in churchgoers (Davis et al., 2023)."

Davis and team report that churchgoers held steady at about that same 47% figure throughout the 20th century. However, in the last 25 years, the trend has reversed. The authors report that the church-going population decreased more than 1.25 times more than the increase in the late 19th century, with over 40 million Americans having left their religion or house of worship. "More people have left the church in the last twenty-five years than all the new people who became Christians" from the first post-revolutionary growth, the second post-civil war period, and the Billy Graham crusades combined (Davis, p. 5-6). All of this despite the fact that under the Reagan administration we added both "in God we trust" to out currency and "under God" to the Pledge of Allegiance.

In 2008 and 2012, Christian theologian Phyllis Tickle wrote two books on what she termed "the Emerging Church." In the first of these, *The Great Emergence*, Tickle said that every 500 years, religion undergoes a major transformation, and she claimed now was once again the time for such a reformation (Tickle, 2008). She said that essentially religions and religious leaders need to have a "rummage sale" wherein they get rid of all the stuff that is no longer relevant to make room for what is coming. For churches, Tickle claimed, that included the buildings and structures—the very essence of what most would identify as the "church."

In her second book on the subject, Tickle (2012) called for the creation of an emergent church. one no longer bound by doctrines, dogmas, or brick-

and-mortar structures. These emergent "churches" were to be out in the communities where people lived and worked. They were to be essentially of the people and for the people. Left behind at the rummage sale would be the need for the church to perpetuate itself for its own survival. Perhaps nothing could have been more prophetic of what is now happening to organized religions.

However, this is not some monolithic movement. To the contrary, there are two opposing movements happening today. While some are leaving organized religion or have never felt a need for any specific doctrine to point the way forward with their spiritual development, there is another segment of the population flocking in droves to more fundamentalist religions. As our society becomes ever more complex, many people cannot tolerate the ambiguity and complexity of postmodern life and seek the simple answers that dualism and fundamentalism offer. One does not have to look far to find examples of these fundamentalist megachurches promising a better life through simple and fundamental aphorisms. Using scriptural excerpts, they promise financial abundance, a cleaner life, and the hope for a heavenly afterlife. For people who are overwhelmed with the complexification of life, those promises sound incredibly appealing. That is not the case for those of us on the spiritual journey. We would prefer a religion that challenges thought and embraces complexity as a catalyst to our spiritual development. But the bottom line is that while disgruntled masses are leaving organized religion, others are moving toward some forms of worship that offer hope.

All in all, people on this spiritual journey did not abandon their spirituality, they just left their religion of origin. The question remains, why? What caused this exodus from organized religion? How are people coming to experience their spirituality and their spiritual growth? Before we address these questions, allow me to point out that I am not setting up some kind of dichotomy between organized religions and spiritual seekers. Many of us who have left the church hold nothing against the religions we know or have been a part of. Further, religions, churches, synagogues, mosques, and ashrams provide many good things for their members: community, ritual, instruction, and pastoral care, among other services. So, religion itself is not bad; it's just that for the seekers, it does not fill the bill for what we need.

In conversations with others on this path, there seem to be four different origins. While all of them have found themselves outside the traditional institution, a few differences separate them.

- One SBNR type is disgruntled with their traditional home or house of worship, including their doctrines, rituals, and dogmas. These are people who are dissatisfied or even repulsed by what they are experiencing in those old forms or singing in some rather militaristic hymns. They may feel labeled as wrong or unbelieving. They don't fit the form, and they don't fit the standards and practices of the traditional home, be it a church, synagogue, or mosque. They felt at odds with the traditional definition of God, Deity, or Universal One. So, out of frustration or just plain disillusionment, they left.

- The second category consists of people who are explorers. It's not so much that they are leaving their religion of origin but that their personal and spiritual development has taken them outside the rubrics of their traditional home. The feel called forward to explore. They perceive worship and spirituality as inward journeys. It's not out there; it's inside. They see prayer not as some kind of conversation with the greater being or some entity apart from themselves but rather as one that opens the pray-er to the experience of some in-dwelling divinity. They seek connection and oneness with that source of life— the life that is living them (not that they are somehow living).

- A third group are those who never grew up in any organized religion. They may have had atheistic or agnostic parents or a family of origin that just never practiced any formalized form of worship. On one level, their path may seem a bit easier in that they don't have a pile of beliefs to deconstruct. Still, they feel a sense of awe and wonder that they cannot shake. Some part of their consciousness knows that there is something bigger and more profound than they are. It is an existential call; an awareness that life is more than eating, sleeping, working, and playing. There must be some greater meaning to life and our interconnectedness with each other. They feel pulled into spirituality, not knowing where they are going or whence that pull is coming. They just know that this is where they must travel.

- The fourth category of explorers on this path are those who for whatever reason do not wish to belong to or affiliate with any organized religion or doctrine. Perhaps it is because the traditional forms of religions do not tolerate their way of being, their sexuality, or their philosophy of life. On the extreme end of this spectrum are those who have been traumatized by their religion, their ministers, or their doctrine/dogma. It was too painful, it couldn't be tolerated, and it just doesn't work anymore; so, they left home. More than not feeling welcome, they have been severely hurt or damaged by the leaders of their religion and often by their families. The caution sign is up because this is a very complex and difficult area of exploration and one that goes far beyond the scope of this text. I neither want to step over the issue of religious trauma nor want to do it a disservice. So, we will name it as it comes up and make reference to other resources where possible.

Just a quick caveat: In mapping out this discussion, I do not wish to characterize religion as "bad" and seeking other forms as "good." That would be a false dichotomy in that for many people religion still can play an important role for them. However, the scope of this book is more about the exploration of spirituality that can happen outside the bounds of traditional religions.

Also, you may experience bits and pieces of any or all of the four dynamics listed above. In fact, feeling both pushed out and pulled forward might be experienced more like having a rocket pack strapped on your back! Nonetheless, the fact remains that, for most of us on this journey, we find ourselves out here (somewhere) in the wilderness. You are there because "out there" is something you are seeking. Out there are unexplored territories ripe for exploration. You are there because of a deep yearning for connection to whatever it is that is greater than yourself. You are there looking for your people and your community. How you (and I) got here is where we want to begin this exploration.

Throughout this book, I will use multiple terms interchangeably to connect with some of the myriad ways spirituality manifests. I may refer to this as a journey, a process, a discovery, or other similar term. I interchangeably use Unity, the One or Oneness, the Divine, Spirit, the Universe, Love, and so on, as descriptors of that Higher Power. While you may not see them as interchangeable, out of respect for others' current state or relative place along that path, I do not wish to assert my experience as either similar to yours or what I believe is some form of the "right" way to do it. There is no right way, only your way. One of the first ground rules of this exploration is that it is uniquely and individually defined and experienced. That was part of why some have left the organized religion; it could not accommodate our individual experience. *But what defines this path and exploration more than anything else is that we each have learned to trust our own experience over that which has been told to us by religious doctrine and family.*

Let's start with the origin and see if we can begin to answer the question of how we got here in the first place.

Leaving Home; I Don't Belong Here

Religions, let's face it, have a point of view and a moral stance, not so much because of the teachings of the founders but more because of those in charge having made a set of judgments in establishing the party line. Perhaps it was because the context of the time was simpler than today. Perhaps the prevailing ethic was so repressive that divergent experiences and beliefs were repressed. Often this was a result of trying to "adhere" to what the original scriptures showed. But often this was done in the name of finding truth. However, just as often it was either misguided or devoid of an understanding of the context and languages in which the original texts were written or of the many languages and translations that had most likely altered some or even in some cases much of the meaning of the original story or its written description.

So, before moving on, let's look at how these doctrines originated. Paul (the former Saul of Tarsus) was the main force in establishing the Christian religion and the many churches in Turkey and Greece.[2] Paul's letters, read in order, clearly show how he was continually refining his understanding of the Divine and of Jesus' divinity. Paul planted hundreds of "churches" throughout the region, but as they attempted to live into his teaching or interpret what Paul had said, it is clear that both their understanding (or misunderstanding) and his ever-evolving theology often created some kind of conflict. So, our own modern-day struggles with church and doctrine are nothing new.

For the first 100 years of Christianity, Christian spirituality was celebrated underground in small groups if only to stay out of view of the oppressive and murderous Roman Empire. But somewhere around the third century in the modern era (CE), the Christian leadership (bishops and cardinals) began gathering for the purposes of creating a systematic theology. What added fuel to this fire was the conversion of Emperor Constantine. When he became Christian, Constantine declared Catholicism to be the religion of the empire, thus elevating its leaders to agents of the ruling class. With the power

---

2. To a lesser extent, Peter and James established their own form of following the teaching in establishing some churches in the Jerusalem region, but it is clear from The Acts of the Apostles that they were not really aligned with Paul. Their focus was on the man Jesus whereas Paul was focused on the divinity of Jesus and what he called the "Body of Christ" often using the term "in Christ" to emphasize that we are all part of that same divinity.

backing of the empire, the ruling bishops and cardinals were able to decree their systemic theology as THE doctrine of Christianity. Jesus moved from a special, half divine/half human unique being to become a Lord and ruler of both the terrestrial world and the underworld. As it was with the Emperor, the rule of Jesus now became unquestionable. And that unquestionable power transferred to his minions: the priests, bishops, cardinals, and above all, the pope.

With this supreme power now in their hands, the power elite of the church began crafting their new version of systematic theology: a way of explaining how all the persons and concepts relating to their understanding of God, Jesus and the universe all fit together as one system. They created the trinitarian philosophy, but in doing so, they had to then resolve the quandary of Jesus's mother, Mary. If Jesus was the all-powerful Son of God, then Mary had to be vested with the same power and status as his mother or even the mother of God. The church leaders had to relate their theological principles to scripture, and where they could find none, they had to create it by adding to the scripture. Additionally, where there were sacred texts that fell outside of their systematic theology, they deleted them from canon.

Here is a simple example of how this rewriting changed the scriptures. The great commission in the Book of Matthew (Mt. 28:19-20) refers to instructions to go out and preach the gospel. The instruction of Jesus was said to be to "make disciples of all people, baptizing them in the name of the Father, Son, and Holy Spirit." But since the trinitarian philosophy had not yet been articulated, it became clear to the early councils that this had to be added into the narrative. Nowhere does Jesus describe himself as the Son of God, claiming instead his humanity as Son of Man. He does refer to the Divine source as the Father, but he extended that relationship to all others. And he did so only to connect those to whom he was preaching with their own divinity. Nonetheless, the priests and bishops of the fourth century councils added in what they felt would substantiate or legitimize theological understanding of the time. And since the trinity was the new message being pushed out by the leadership, they most likely added those words to the Matthew text— something that is noticeably missing from the synoptic gospels.

Rewriting sacred texts is not new or unique to the early Christian fathers (300+ CE). The Hebrew scriptures were rewritten—with major revisions— at least four times. These revisionists were called the Jahwists, the Elohists, the Deuteronomists, and the Priestly writers (though biblical scholars don't use those distinctions much anymore). Each of the "official" writers not only scribed their own books to be added to the sacred texts, but more important, they also revised the other texts and oral traditions to fit the theology of their time. It is a theme as old as religion itself.

Beyond the scriptures, we have the rituals and hymns of our religions. The original hymns were variations on the Psalms, such as the antiphonal chants of the Gregorian monks. As music became a central part of the religious experience, theology was written into our hymnody. Like the Psalms, hymns fall into several categories: praise, confession, lament, thanksgiving, encouragement and proclamation. Though many of the early Christianity's hymns have been lost or discarded along the way, the Church has continued the tradition, adding hymns to the collection since the Gregorian age of the nineth and tenth centuries.

However, for those who have felt that they had to leave their religion, the feeling of not belonging goes well beyond the subtleties of theology and doctrine embedded in these hymns. For me, the first memory I had of not belonging came in the form of a hymn. Written in 1858, "Stand Up, Stand Up for Jesus" was a popular hymn in the Lutheran church in which I grew up. We Lutherans would proudly rise to our feet and belt out the lyrics:

Stand up, stand up for Jesus,
Ye soldiers of the cross;
Lift high His royal banner—
It must not suffer loss.
From victory unto victory
His army shall He lead,
Till every foe is vanquished,
And Christ is Lord indeed.

Perhaps it was because our church had so many WWII veterans who may have related to the warring analogy in the lyrics; perhaps it just was a good rousing melody that the organist could pound out with swell and great pedals to the floor (we Lutherans loved our pipe organs). For whatever reason, it was a regular at our church, and I was fairly certain, even at that age, that it had nothing whatsoever to do with Jesus's teachings of peace and love of one's enemies (our foes) or of humility and surrender. I was only about ten or maybe 12, but I already had a fascination with religion and theology. Yet, somehow, I could not relate to the depth of ego, pride and imperialism woven into this so-called hymn. "Stand Up for Jesus," "The Battle Hymn of the Republic" and others like them were the first nudges toward the exit doors of my religion of origin. For those of us in this group of seekers, it wasn't so much that we have been forced out the door, it was more like we can no longer stay with the traditional doctrines and confines inside the building.

The bottom line is that, from the beginning of when the church became part of the power structure of society, religions have been infused with concepts and constructs of imperial power, of hierarchical power, and of subservient followers—peasants and peons, if you will—who were at the total mercy of the ruling class; who in turn thought of themselves as next to godly and angelic. The Christian church leaders created a system of canonizing "saintly" leaders and martyrs of the (Catholic) church, further devaluing the common worshipper as nothing more than worms and unforgiven, hopeless sinners.

They were the ones who reinterpreted the teachings of the masters and who infused scriptures, rituals, and hymns with their often-unconscious biases of the masculine power elite. It is no wonder why so many have chosen to leave. We had to go!

Outgrowing Home: A Developmental Quandary

I would wager (though I have no statistical evidence) that the largest group of spiritually homeless are not those who felt pushed out of the church but those who have chosen to leave their former houses of worship because of their own moral/ethical development outgrowing the stagnant rigidity of their religion of origin. From a purely developmental perspective, this could be expected. We humans develop our moral/ethical thinking along certain predictable paths[3]. Stage theorists and developmental psychologists contend that we move through various phases of understanding of life and of ourselves. Ultimately the process of developing a self-concept and a sense of self-esteem produces a systematic understanding of the world and one's place within it, as well as forming the framework for our moral and ethical decision-making.

However, the problem in that is that religions, and those who preach their doctrines, do not evolve and mature with us. Briefly, we can think of our developmental pathway as moving from our childhood understanding or the world in dualistic terms to the complex understanding of life we hold as adults. As children we learn in duality—like all those opposites books we read to our children. You know the ones: good/bad, big/little, dark/light and so on. But eventually this nice demarcation of things and their opposites can't explain gradients in between those opposites, and we move to a new level of understanding called multiplicity.

In multiplicity, there is still an ultimate good or bad, but now we understand that there are shades of good and bad. Black and white still exist, but we now

---

3. See Chapter 8, The Path of Spiritual Evolution, for a detailed explanation of the seven stages of spiritual/moral development.

understand that there are shades of gray in between. Morally, we understand right and wrong, but we can see where it is sometimes possible to have a justifiable wrong. Or we can understand that someone we thought was a bad person could do good—things that cannot make sense in a dualistic world view. And so, all is well until dualism no longer can make sense of more confusing and complex distinctions.

Unfortunately, the same fate awaits multiplicity. It can only work for so long. Somewhere along the line, things start showing up as neither good nor bad—it's just that someone else has made that judgment. At this point, our thinking evolves into one of two states, either nihilism or contextual relativism. In nihilism, we think that there is no good or bad, no right or wrong; it just is. And in contextualism, we extend that concept to say that though there is no good or bad, perhaps the situation is what deems one choice as the right thing to do. It is what is happening when our teenaged children plead that "everyone else is doing it," so why can't they? Fortunately, these sibling stages of nihilism and relativism are short-lived.

Finally, we arrive at the very sophisticated state as adults where we understand that there is no right, no wrong; that there even isn't a great difference between you and me. Ninety-nine-point-nine percent of our DNA is identical; we really are all one. We realize that it is our choice to determine what is right and wrong for us to do, based on a mature understanding of all things we have learned thus far. And at the same time, we have learned that we cannot force our morals on others, knowing that they must also come to their own conclusions.

But here is the problem: doctrine most often does not evolve. Much of it stays at fundamental dualism and peddles easy-to-understand platitudes and moral codes. The religions fail at helping us grow and evolve our own thinking because they are firmly stuck in a pattern of belief that there is an ultimate right and wrong that governs all things. A more Machiavellian view would be that a religion adheres to dualism because it is the easiest to control and thereby the easiest way to control its people.

Thus, it becomes inevitable that, as we develop along our path, we find less and less support from the religion and religious leaders. Of course, there are many ministers, rabbis and imams who are themselves mature in their moral development, but who are bound to the doctrine that dictates that they must preach to the most simple and common thought pattern. I have had and continue to have many wonderful discussions with clergy who understand the world from a highly evolved place. And of course, that is a great feeling of fellowship. But when the sabbath rolls around, they find that they have to preach to the masses or to the least common denominator. When it comes to finding our community, our people and our home, the religion itself, including its agents and ritual prayers, its hymns and scriptures, remains dualistic and even tribal as a culture.

Beth is a brilliant scholar and lawyer. She grew up in the Jewish tradition and learned to question everything as part of her Talmudic studies. After earning her JD, she went to work on issues of social justice. She worked with the Southern Poverty Law Center in the late 70's which was still dealing with the aftermath of the civil rights movement. She affiliated with the American Civil Liberties Union defending individual's rights to due process and free speech. Beth saw between the lines of right and wrong or good and bad. Her work took her well down the developmental path and resulted in moving far beyond even her roots of Judaism, arriving at a place by her mid-forties of understanding that surpassed much of her original teachings. She told me once, "I can't go back—there is no reverse gear in development. And there is no way I can fit conveniently back in that box that used to be so comforting to me." Though she still considers herself to be "deeply spiritual," she does not affiliate with any particular religion or attend any house of worship but follows what she considers more of a Buddhist path of spirituality.

This developmental path is not confined to any particular religion or theology. It is just that at some point we feel that it is in our own best interest to leave the religion of our youth. We have outgrown it. Like that favorite shirt or pair of shoes you had as a kid, you just grew out of them. There need be no judgment in that statement. It is the simple truth that those who have pushed forward with their development find that earlier beliefs and creeds no longer fit as simple absolutes.

The dual problem in this developmental mismatch is that our development is usually precipitated by tough experiences, failures, catastrophes, and existential crises. But it is often those same issues that normally would drive people to seek answers in their religion or through their faith tradition. (I had a professor in seminary who contended that all religion was based on pain and grief.) When a seeker has lost faith in the religion's ability to provide any assistance or support, there are scant few places to turn, throwing their spiritual practice into a tailspin. Later, in Chapter Eight, I will discuss the developmental path and how one's view of god/the universe/power and such notions evolve over the various stages and states of development.

The Explorers (who never had a home)

The third grouping of spiritually homeless are those who perhaps never belonged to a sect, religious denomination, or worship community. Yet as typical humans, they have felt a sense of something greater than themselves. They sense that there is something transcendent that is more than the sum of people, animals, plants, and the earth. This feeling is as old as human beings themselves. For example, some of the earliest cave drawings found in the caves of France date back nearly 30,000 years. Some of the paintings show a man lying on his back gazing skyward at what looks like a wild bull but which archeologists now believe were depictions of constellations, indicating that these early homo-sapiens were fascinated with the skies and had a working knowledge of astrology.

But we need not look back to antiquity to know the raw truth of this. Who hasn't gotten goose bumps staring up at a star-filled night sky or the beautiful deep red-orange of a sunset fading to the indigo of an evening sky? For me, it has always been waterfalls. Whether a small cascade in the Appalachian Mountains or the unfathomable power and size of Victoria Falls, the sights and sounds of waterfalls somehow resonate with something deep within my heart and soul. When visiting Victoria Falls a few decades ago, I was first impressed by the fact that there is no one vantage point—not even a thousand feet up in a helicopter—where one can see the entirety of the falls. In the sky, you can't see how deep it is, but you are amazed that the Zambezi at that point is a mile wide. But walking along the unguarded edge of the opposing cliff facing the falls, you have no way of telling, as you walk along, how much farther it goes. As I was taking in this wonder, two teenaged boys ran past me, joking and shoving each other. One misstep and they would have fallen 350 feet to the bottom of the gorge! But they quickly passed beyond my view. I had almost forgotten about the boys as I continued along the path, searching my mind for enough adjectives and expletives to describe what I was seeing, until I arrived at the eastern cataract. I had totally run out of words to describe the beauty, force, and grandeur of this mammoth cascade. And sitting there, speechless and motionless in their experience sat the two boys, perhaps in their own way trying to fathom this power and beauty. The Smoke That Thunders, as the native name describes it, had enveloped us all in awe.

Awe and wonder go hand in hand in inspiring spirituality. But what of those who have no context of spirituality or have never had a religious vocabulary? Barbara grew up in a family that had never gone to any type of worship services in at least two generations. Her dad was a scientist and contended that only the observable could be real and since God and "those religious things," as he called them, could neither be seen or proven, they must not be real. Barbara just took that at face value as she was growing up. She too became a scientist (choosing mechanical engineering in college) and thought nothing of religion until late in her twenties. She tells of a time when she was backpacking through the Colorado Rockies as part of an Outward Bound program. On the third night of the program, the participants began their solo experience during which they were to speak to no one (if anyone were to be encountered along the trail) and remain silent for the next two days. The weather was perfect, and so instead of pitching her tent, she decided to sleep under the stars.

As she lay there just taking in the wonder of a starry night that had no interference from ambient light in any direction, she was overwhelmed with feelings. First, she says, she was hit with a sense of fear and impending doom. It didn't seem to come from anywhere in particular, but it was as real as any fear she had ever experienced. The fear morphed into a sense of deep loneliness and sadness. She said that she began to weep and then broke into the most cathartic crying session she can ever remember. Once again, she tried to identify where in her body the sadness had come from, but it seemed to be a whole-body experience. Then, just as she finally stopped crying, she says she felt a warmth come over her body Despite being at about 9,000 feet in elevation where the air temperature was rather chilling, she felt warm. This time she was able to place the source of the warmth as it radiated from her core, her solar plexus, and heart.

Barbara said she laid back on her sleeping bag, spreadeagle, arms and legs wide open to the side. It felt to her as though she was being bathed in light, and, as dark as the night was, she was able to see all around her as if she were the light source illuminating the rocks and bushes. Barbara told me that the feeling she had at that moment was one of total connection. She felt like she was a star, that she was part of the cosmos, and yet she felt so connected to the ground and earth holding her there that she sensed that she was almost transparent, that sky and earth were connected *through* her. She told me that it was the most profoundly spiritual experience of her life and that ever since she considered herself to be a spiritual person.

Interestingly, one set of studies by the Pew Research group (2015) found that people who were regular church-goers[4] were less likely to have spiritual or religious experiences like Barbara had, suggesting alternatively, that non-affiliated persons might be more likely to have such experiences than their more religiously "observant" peers. Said another way, the great mythologist, Joseph Campbell once noted that the best way to ensure that you will *not* have a spiritual experience is to have studied (theology) beforehand. For those who have never practiced religion or attended religious services, their landscape is a clean slate, unencumbered by any notion of what it should be or look like.

Of course, not all the "unchurched" have religious or spiritual experiences. Many go happily along through life without any interest in having such experiences. What is interesting is that almost to a person, this group described spirituality as a transcendent experience, that is, that it moves them beyond a sense of separateness to one of unity with everything. And that everything is so far beyond comprehension that it includes a sense of the Divine. For many adherents to a particular religion, God has been presented as an other-worldly being "out there" as opposed to what current theology holds as ubiquitous, including within each of us individually.

No Thanks (Spiritual Abuse and Religious Trauma)

In discussing the subject of the spiritual but not religious, I have come across several individuals who for various reasons want nothing to do with organized religions. They see what religions have done in the name of their doctrines and/or dogmas and want nothing to do with whatever that is. A segment of the group that eschew religions are those who have been severely mistreated by their religion of origin to the level of being fully traumatized. For them, living with Post Traumatic Stress (PTSD) is a reality and churches, religious

---

4. While both Davis, et al. and the Pew Research group professes to be non-sectarian, I want to acknowledge that the terms church and churchgoers are particularly Christian terms and may not be reflective of other religions.

doctrines, dogmatic beliefs or anything related to them can trigger severe stress reactions. So, let's address this elephant in the room first.

⚠ DANGER DEEP WATER Let me say from the start that this is a very complex issue and one that falls way beyond the scope of this book. So, let me tread lightly and claim that I have no authority on the subject nor any desire to misrepresent its many nuanced elements. Though I do know many who would fall into this category, I cannot begin to understand the depths of their pain and trauma or the horrors of their lived experiences. What I understand of trauma, as learned from my profession, is that trauma has a way of fracturing the experience, and in doing so, fractures parts of our personhood.

Spiritual abuse and religious trauma can result from a number of sources. It can be as simple as being forced into certain "religious" beliefs or being required to adhere to a credo as happens in many cult-like "churches." The perpetrators use guilt and shame to control behavior and often employ fear-based teachings as a means of control. Often abuse involves the use of scriptures or scriptural references either to shame a person or to "protect" an abusive person or relationship. Quite often people report being gaslit to manipulate their reality and personal perceptions of abuse. And in many cases the abuse is amplified by denying the individual who is suffering any choice in decision-making about their fate. They feel not only abused physically, mentally and emotionally, but also the trauma induced by having no escape route of choice to defend themselves only makes it more intolerable. As a result, the traumatized individual feels guilt, shame, and outright terror which easily gets turned inward as low self-esteem or self-loathing.

While PTSD has more recently been included in the Diagnostic and Statistical Manual of Mental Disorders (DSM-5), religious trauma and spiritual abuse have yet to be included among the causes of PTSD. Nonetheless, in talking with several close friends, this sort of trauma is no less debilitating that that which is suffered by combat veterans. In addition to recurrent and triggered traumatic stress, victims report a wide variety of other effects like constant fear, depression, panic attacks, rage and anger, dissociative disorders (not feeling connected to reality) and general emotional isolation of flat affect.

Aditionally, because of the entrapment that is often a part of religious trauma and spiritual abuse, it is often difficult for victims to escape such religious groups. It is no wonder that these fellow seekers and explorers want nothing to do with any organized religion or group. What is amazing, though, is that despite it all, people who have been victimized and abused by their religion and religious leaders may still experience a deep spirituality of their own. Similar to the stories about the torture of John of the Cross (described in Chapter Six on the Dark Night of the Soul), repression, abuse, and trauma may be associated with a person's religion of origin or the leaders of a spiritual practice, but rather than destroying their spiritual beliefs, it results in their not wanting to be associated with the practices and ways of that religion. Like so many explorers on the spiritual path, even people who have been severely traumatized may still trust their guts over that which was being forced on them by their religion. Obviously, these are extreme examples, but I wanted to name them as a significant factor in why many have chosen to leave organized religions behind.

In the realm of sexuality and partnering, there has always been a significant percentage of the population throughout the ages that were gay, lesbian and trans or gender fluid. In many cultures, that was just accepted as what was— not judging it as normal or abnormal, but simply accepting those differences. Peter is gay, something he had always known since he was a kid. So, he never tried to hide it growing up. Unfortunately, not only did it result in his being beaten up by the school bullies, it also made him a pariah from the church his family attended. As a young man he began searching the Bible for references to homosexuality, finding Jonathan's love of David to be an inspiration (1 Samuel: 18-20). But when he presented that to the pastor, he was met with stern rebuke. That set Peter off on a search for a spiritual home that would accept him as he was. Despite always knowing himself to be gay, those around him made homosexuality a dirty word and something that was clearly wrong with him. He knew that he believed in a loving and accepting God and felt that there was nothing wrong with him. It wasn't until Peter came across an open Unitarian Universalist congregation in New England that he found that home. There he was able to marry his long-time lover and become an active member of that spiritual community.

Others may not have been as fortunate as Peter, though he claims that his "good fortune" was a result of his determined search. Marriage for our queer siblings continues to be one of the many sticking points that could drive them out. But since the dominant Christian sect, the Catholic Church, had elevated marriage to the level of sacred/sacramental, Christian leaders felt the need to define just what that sacred bond was. The problem that existed within that process of sanctifying marriage is that it was being decreed by a group of celibate and sometimes covertly (or closeted) gay men. Perhaps having the difficulty of resolving their own sexuality with their theology, or for some other reason, they declared that a marriage shall be limited to a union between a man and a woman, and further, that sex was to be for procreation alone. That wasn't wrong in itself, but it certainly excluded all other forms of coupling and sexual expressions.

If you are among those who fall into the category of spiritual abuse and religious trauma, there are many resources and treatment modalities that can help. A few of these are various forms of trauma-informed therapies: Cognitive-Behavioral Therapy (CBT), dialectal behavior therapy (similar to CBT), and EMDR or eye-movement desensitization. More likely than not, you may know of and have explored other treatments, and I strongly advise that you shop around to find what is right for you.

And a last subdivision of the "no thank you" group are those witnesses to the folly and abuses of organized religions. While they may not have suffered any of the above-mentioned abuses, they clearly see the damage done and want no part in tacitly condoning those horrors by affiliating with any religion or religious group. They often are allies for others victimized by organized religion; they serve as advocates for adults who as children were psychologically and sexually abused by priests, ministers, and religious leaders, often calling to account even the organizations who have turned a blind eye to those abuses. This group is just as deeply spiritual as the others but do not wish to be a part of anything close to what they perceive as endemic to the power abuses resulting from such authority. They see that once the Church was made a part of the power elite in the fourth century, that power began to infect the leadership of the religions, something that has only gotten worse over the centuries.

To be certain, there are also many others who come from churched backgrounds or who have never been affiliated with a religion or who want nothing to do with those religions they have seen or known about. People who have evolved their spirituality outside of any religious group or organized religion feel that their spirituality is quite personal and often feel no need for that experience to be blessed or sanctioned by some religious body. Like all mystics, they own and fully validate their personal experiences of spirituality. They represent the truth that humans tend to wonder about things beyond themselves. They have a sense of awe about the world, about others, nature, and life in general. To them, everything points to spirituality—everything, that is except religions. Those they often describe as getting in the way of spiritual experience. These spiritual explorers, like many of us on this journey, have evolved in their spiritual beliefs and work regularly and consciously on their spiritual development.

Numinodiversity

I needed a way to describe the territory of this work and could not find any appropriate word. Numinodiversity is made up, but so was neurodiversity at one time! The root of the word is *numinous,* meaning something that has a strong spiritual quality; it describes an experience that makes you both fearful and fascinated, awed and attracted at the same time. Numinous is the strong personal feeling of being overwhelmed and inspired. But this feeling or state, if you will, is not monolithic or even commonly shared. It is, in fact, unique to each individual, hence the suffix of diversity. Numinodiversity is an umbrella term that refers to the myriad variations in how the spiritual aspects of life are experienced. And numinodivergence, therefore, is the awareness of the many and varied ways in which Spirit and the Divine are both experienced and expressed.

In writing *Spiritually Homeless*, I want to be sensitive to both that diversity and to your spiritual health. Healthy spirituality by my understanding is the state of having meaning in one's life; of having a sense of connection to something that is larger than oneself. Spiritual health connotes having a sense of purpose and connection with self, others, nature, and the transcendent or divine. We will discuss elements of each of these throughout the book

Journaling: Which type of explorer are you and what was the catalyst for your stepping onto this path of spirituality? What were the pivotal points that moved you forward or away from your initial beliefs? Did you feel pushed out, just outgrew your religion, or is your spiritual quest something totally unique to you, having not arrived there because of any prior religious experiences? Reflect and write a bit about the trajectory of your spiritual journey.

CHAPTER THREE

It never occurred to me, because no one ever told me, that I would one day as a minister stop believing – stop believing in God as I once had, stop believing in the religion that I had been practicing most of my life, stop believing in what I was doing, stop believing that my life as a minister, professor of Bible, and writer made any sense. Had I been warned that this day was coming, I might have been more careful.

Renita J Weems, *Listening for God*

Losing Our Way
(exploring without a compass)

For where we are going, there is no actual map—you know the kind with roads and street names, towns and villages, and certainly no expressway for getting from here to there. By the same token, we must pack light, carry nothing extra, "just in case" because all of that "stuff" is only to provide some kind of false assurance that we can make it on our own. Later on in Weems' book, she warns, "those who wish to find themselves must first be willing to lose themselves. Only when we risk getting lost do we find our way, and only when we stop trying to see our footsteps does our pathway become more certain."

Whether we are leaving a particular house of worship or religious belief behind or venturing out on our own to solve some mystery, the truth of the matter is that we have set out on a journey *through* mystery. When I was younger and exploring various religions, I recall attending some Catholic churches, and somewhere in the service just before the Eucharist, the priest would repeat the words that represented "the great mystery," saying that Christ was born, died, and will rise again. I remember thinking in my Protestant naïveté, "that's not really a mystery if you are certain enough of it to repeat it every Sunday!" It may have been a statement of belief, but it sounded as certain as someone saying the sun will rise tomorrow. The real mystery was that I had no clue what was going on. I had only a feeling of unrest, curiosity, and wonderment. But there were no breadcrumbs on the trail and often there was not even a trail to follow. I was alone in the woods, lost with no compass, guidebook, or clues as to where I was heading or what was "there" if and when I actually got there.

For centuries, traditional frameworks for connecting to God have relied on objectifying or localizing the Divine. God has often been described as a being who resides in a particular place—the heavens, the temple, or even within the confines of a church. These frameworks gave many people a sense of stability and direction. They provided rituals, doctrines, and sacred texts that functioned as spiritual maps, guiding believers toward God. However, for those who have stepped outside these frameworks—whether due to doubt, trauma, or a natural evolution of faith—these maps no longer point to a place that feels real.

The challenge with such maps is that they often treat God as something "other"—a being we approach, encounter, and petition, rather than a reality woven into the fabric of our existence. These frameworks depend on certainty: God is "here," and if you do these things or believe this doctrine, you will meet God. But what happens when those certainties unravel? When prayers seem unanswered, rituals feel hollow, and the promised presence of God feels absent? The old maps, once so reliable, can feel like they're charting a land that no longer exists.

Much of this disillusionment comes from the way traditional frameworks localize God—placing divinity in specific places, objects, or events. In many traditions, God's presence is tied to sacred spaces: the sanctuary, the altar, the Eucharistic elements. While these practices can indeed facilitate profound encounters with the Divine, they can also inadvertently create a sense that God is confined to these spaces. Once a person steps outside of the church, physically or spiritually, they may feel like they've left God behind, leading to a sense of spiritual homelessness.

Even language itself can contribute to the problem. When we speak of God as Father, King, or Shepherd, these metaphors can be deeply meaningful, but they can also shape our expectations of God as someone who behaves like a human figure, intervening in our lives as a parent or ruler might. Over time, these images risk becoming rigid, leaving little room for a God who transcends all categories. If God does not behave like the loving father or the just king we were taught to expect, it can feel as though God has disappeared—or never existed at all.

The discomfort with these traditional frameworks is not a rejection of faith but a recognition of their limits. They were never meant to contain God, only to point toward the Divine. As the mystic and poet Rainer Maria Rilke observed, "For staying is nowhere." God is not an endpoint on a map but the infinite reality that defies all boundaries. For those who have left church maps behind, this can feel terrifying—like losing one's way in the wilderness. But it can also open the possibility of discovering the Divine in new and unexpected ways, unbound by human constructions.

This moment of disorientation is a pivotal stage of spiritual growth. It invites us to question whether the old maps were ever about finding God at all, or if they were about making us feel secure in our journey. What if God is not "out there" to be found but is instead the love that permeates all things—the ground of being, the heartbeat of existence? While losing the old maps can feel like we are lost, perhaps we are being invited into a deeper trust—a trust that God is present even in the uncharted wilderness.

For many on this path, losing our way is a conscious choice; a choice to go off the beaten path. It's like Frost's familiar poem *The Road Not Taken*. Frost writes how he stood there looking as far as he could down each road and then very conscientiously decided to take the one no one else had taken. Though he reserved the right to return and take the other, he knew that he probably would never get back to that decision point. These choices that some of us have made, to leave and go our separate way, are much the same. We know that the building may still be standing there if we ever want to return, but like Frost, we "doubted if [we] should ever come back."

Others, like my friend Paula, woke up one day depressed. Her melancholy did not seem to be attached to anything in particular. It was just as if life had become dull and tasteless. In a matter of just a few weeks she said goodbye to her live-in boyfriend and packed her bags, landing in an ashram in India. There she studied under the Guru and did chores around the ashram for two years. The structure was nice as it kept her mind occupied. Her meditation practice improved, but that was about the length and breadth of it. Then, when the guru insisted that she have sex with him, she knew it was time to leave. Her beliefs and trust in another spiritual practice had been destroyed. Coming back to America, she made enough for an apartment and food by a series of odd jobs everything from shining shoes in Faneuil Hall to crewing sail boats along the Atlantic coast. Though the sadness had left her, she said she still felt empty. So having cobbled enough money together to enroll in a personal transformation course, she tried another direction. Eventually, she took every course or workshop on personal improvement that she could, but nothing did the trick.

One day she as was meditating, she had what she calls a spiritual awakening. She suddenly realized that what was missing in her life was a sense of spirituality not church or a religious community, just her belief in some kind of Higher Power. She had always believed in a Higher Power, as she says, "Sometimes it looked like God and sometimes the Universe itself," but she had lost it along the way. Her family of origin was Pentecostal, which she still enjoyed because of the singing, but the "whole talking in tongues and the Jesus thing" didn't call to her. Her search began by going to different types of religious services, eventually finding her path in the Universal Life church.

Obviously, many lose their way and have not yet found the path out of the woods or even found some sort of trail blazes left behind by other explorers. So, what do we do when we get lost? Is lost a place of spirituality, or is it one devoid of all senses? Getting lost (or perhaps more accurately, discovering that we are lost) is perhaps a bit like the journey through what is called "the dark night of the soul," which will be discussed in later chapters. But for many it is just a place of confusion and nothingness. We begin asking unanswerable questions like "How did I get here?"

I call them unanswerable questions because the only answer is that we have traveled a path whether a logic train of thoughts or as a result of a series of seemingly random events that resulted in our being right here in this spot at this particular time. So, quizzing ourselves on why and how is relatively or totally useless. "Ah," say some resisters, "but isn't it important to know cause and effect so I don't repeat the same error?" Perhaps. But the bottom line is that you are still here, and here is where we must begin the job of getting more conscious of what is going on spiritually within you.

Ego is very intent in making logical sense out of everything, but Spirit and Soul are not concerned with logic at all. Spiritual growth starts with becoming present with the here and now, with acceptance of what "is" right now. What is happening? What am I feeling? What is true for me in this moment?

"The change of life is the time when you meet yourself at a crossroads and you decide whether to be honest or not before you die," wrote Katharine Burler Hathaway (Hathaway, 2000). The truth is what is discovered when we actually choose to be honest and begin to see things as they are not as we think or hope they are.

That is not as easily done as it is to say. Given that our minds are the meaning-making machines that they are, most likely what we think we see or what we think is going on inside and outside of ourselves has already been interpreted by our minds. Those interpretations are derived by the stored memories and information the mind has accumulated so far in life. In other words, we are looking at the present events through a filter of our own making, based on our previous experience. It is much like trying to see out of a very dirty window. What you see out there is fuzzy, clouded, and partially obscured by the dirt, dust, and haze on the dirty window. In fact, some things that are right there in front of us we might not even see because they are still obscure or we do not think that they are there or should not be there.

I often tell the story of a friend of mine who is married to a financial manager who believes that money is abundant and everywhere to be found. My friend, however, believes that if someone dropped money, they would obviously stop and pick it up, or if they got home and discovered it missing, would go back out, retracing their path in order to find the lost dollar bill. What is interesting is that every time they went out for an evening date, his wife was always stopping to pick up money; a quarter here, a dollar there and once even a twenty-dollar bill. Yet, he swears that he never sees it until she picks it up. How is it possible that two people of substantial intelligence can both look at the same territory and see it differently? The simple answer is that they have differing expectations of what they will see or not see.

When we apply this example to our spiritual experience, we must recognize that what we are seeing or not seeing and what we make that mean is almost entirely dependent on what our minds are willing to see and what our minds interpret that to mean. It may take years of training for us to see past our biases and interpretation making. But what if we begin to think of Spirit not as an entity but as love itself love that is abundantly everywhere and yet not confined to anywhere in particular?

To say that God is love is both profoundly comforting and yet deeply disorienting. Love is something we recognize in our relationships, in acts of kindness, in the beauty of the natural world. Yet, when we speak of God as love itself—abstract, amorphous, and ubiquitous, it challenges our very understanding of what it means to relate to the Divine. How can we connect with something that has no boundaries, no form, and no single location? God as love is both everywhere and nowhere, present in all things but eluding our grasp. This paradox is one that mystics, poets, and spiritual thinkers have wrestled with for centuries.

The Christian mystic Julian of Norwich captured this tension beautifully when she wrote, *"God is the ground of our beseeching."* Julian speaks of a God who is not merely external to us but intimately entwined with our very being—a love so vast it is the foundation of existence itself including our existence. When Julian says it is the ground of our beseeching, she is essentially saying that which you are seeking is what causes your seeking in the first place. Yet this same God, she acknowledges, cannot be fully known or contained by human thought. Similarly, Meister Eckhart, the 14th-century Dominican theologian, challenges us to let go of our desire to define God: *"God is not found in the soul by adding anything, but by a process of subtraction."* To encounter the God of love, Eckhart suggests, we must relinquish our need for certainty and control, strip away what we think we know, embracing the mystery of a presence that cannot be named.

This paradox of God as love also finds expression in the poetry of Rainer Maria Rilke. In his *Duino Elegies*, Rilke writes of a love that both sustains and overwhelms us: *"For beauty is nothing but the beginning of terror, which we are still just able to endure."* Rilke's words suggest that to encounter the Divine is to stand at the edge of something vast and unknowable—a love so infinite that it defies comprehension. This love, Rilke implies, is not something we can possess; it is something we must surrender into.

Even Rumi, the Sufi mystic, invites us into this paradoxical understanding of God. In his poetry, Rumi often describes love as both the path and the destination, the seeker and the sought. For Rumi, God as love is not a distant deity to be approached; it is the very force that moves us, draws us, and transforms us. This love is present in all things, yet it calls us to move beyond ourselves, to step into the unknown.

The challenge for spiritual seekers is that this kind of love does not conform to our expectations. Humans long for a God who feels tangible, who meets us on our terms. But God as love does not dwell in a single place or moment; it is everywhere and nowhere. This can feel like an absence, yet it is an absence that makes space for the fullness of Divine presence.

This paradox of Divine love invites us into a new way of being—one that moves beyond certainty and control into the realm of trust and surrender. To encounter God as love is not to find a fixed point of reference but to be immersed in a reality that is all-encompassing and ever-expanding. It is to see the Divine not as an object to be approached but as the very ground of our existence, the source of all connection and meaning. As the theologian Paul Tillich wrote, *"The name of infinite and inexhaustible depth and ground of all being is God. That depth is what the word 'God' means (Tillich, 1948, p. 57)." Call it God, Spirit, or the Divine or whatever you wish – it is all just an attempt to give Love a name.*

For those who have left the old maps behind, this understanding of God as love can feel both liberating and unsettling. It demands a willingness to live with ambiguity, to trust that the Divine is present even when it feels absent. But it also offers a profound hope: that in the vast, boundless reality of God as love, we are never truly alone. Instead, we are always being drawn deeper into the mystery of a love that is everywhere and nowhere, calling us to transformation.

It is possible to feel lost without actually being lost. We can feel touched by the Divine whether or not that has happened in some way. We interpret information that doesn't fit our current operating paradigm as "confusing" and turn away from it because it doesn't make sense. When I am conducting spirituality workshops, I frequently send people out into the world to find something of interest that has caught their attention. When they return to the room, I ask them to tell the group what they see in the object they noticed and to describe its qualities. Then, after each person has described their interesting object, I ask them to again describe it only to substitute the word "I" for the object. For example, a person may have noticed the beautiful green moss growing on a rotting stump, describing the way the old is giving birth to the new life. In restating that example they then would say that their old ways of being are dying and giving birth to their new qualities and ways of being. By doing so, not only do they see how their perception was filtered by their self-concepts but also gain new and sometimes profound insights into themselves.

Journaling: Where and when do you feel most lost? Take some time to think about the times when you felt most confused about your beliefs. What was the source of your confusion or lost feeling? What beliefs were you letting go of and what about your spiritual truth felt off or wrong?

CHAPTER FOUR

There are certain truths that can be known only if we are sufficiently emptied, sufficiently ready, sufficiently confused, or sufficiently destabilized. That's the genius of it all.

Richard Rohr, *Things Hidden*

Being Pulled Forward

Many, perhaps the majority, of people I have talked with say that they don't really know why they feel compelled to follow this path. Some call it a strange force. Others call it Spirit or God. But many of us refer to it as a sense of curiosity. What is out there? Why are we here? What is my purpose? What is it that I long for, really? These and so many other questions lay at the source of our seeking.

Sometimes it seems to me to be almost a morbid curiosity, like the kind of feeling you have when watching the video of a plane crash. You don't really want to watch but then again, you can't seem to pull away from it. There is no way I really want to move forward with this journey and at the same time I almost have no other choice – it's what I must do. So, we are pulled into the next moment and the next one after that.

What do you believe is urging you forward and toward what is it that you are moving? These questions haunt us. Many times, I forget that I am on a quest, or perhaps it's more like I pretend not to know what I am seeking. The questions seem unanswerable, so I try to forget that I live inside a question at all. Of course, I am not the prototype, nor do I even think that I should be. This is just my experience.

Since I have always had an interest in why people believe what they believe, I have interviewed or casually asked hundreds of folks those two questions. The most frequent responses center around some form of spiritual experience. They hear something, see something, or feel something and, like a curious child, start looking for the source. "What was that sound?" "Where is it coming from?" And so, they start poking around in the dark, looking around the corners, trying to find any clues as to what is calling them or beckoning them forward.

One of the grandfathers of the field of psychology, William James (1842-1910), delivered a series of lectures which he titled "The Varieties of Religious Experience." James felt that spirituality and religion were elements of human nature. In his introductory lecture, he said that if he were to characterize "the life of religion in its broadest and most general terms possible, one might say that it consists of the belief that there is an unseen order, and that our supreme good lies in harmoniously adjusting ourselves thereto (James, 2022, p. 22)." In further lectures, he went about classifying these experiences into five categories. Those were: Mystical Experiences, Conversion Experiences, Saintliness, Feelings of Dependence, and the Healthy-Minded versus Sick Soul experience. Of these, most people with whom I spoke refer to the first two. While much research and many studies on religion, spirituality, religious cults, and other experiences have been conducted since the dawn of the field in James' time, he still seems to have zeroed in on a few salient issues. For the purposes of our discussion, we will cherry-pick from James' discussions of mystical and conversion experiences.

Mystical experiences, according to James, are characterized by a sense of unity with the Divine or with the universal. They often result in a feeling of oneness, maybe not at first but as the mystical experience unfolds there seems to be an experience of the transcendence of time and space. Mystical experiences transport a person to sensing the ineffable. It is a feeling or a sensing that defies any description, but they are at the same time imbued with a sense of peace or understanding.

James goes on to explain that there are four earmarks of the mystical experience. The first is that it is ineffable. That is, it is felt and somehow understood yet has qualities that cannot be put into words, that "it defies expression, that no adequate report of its contents can be given in words (James, 2022, p. 122)." Those who have had such "conversations with God" as Neale Donald Walsch called them, feel embarrassed sometimes by their inability to express what it felt like or what meaning they had affixed to their experiences. However ineffable they may be, the second characteristic of mystical experiences is that they possess what James called a noetic quality. That is, however they are experienced, the individual is left with a sense of insight into or revelation of some greater truth. Last, James felt that mystical experiences were often short-lived or transient and essentially passive that the person felt the experience had happened to them rather than by their own volition.

Conversion experiences involve a transformation of a person's beliefs, attitudes, and life direction. These can be sudden, gradual, or what James called the educational variety. Unlike mystical experiences, conversion experiences can be volitional, where a person is actively seeking transformation. These are the folks who I often refer to as seekers, who like me, have been on a path of discovery for some time. Through our efforts to learn and discover what lies beyond the traditional teachings of the Church, we have begun to piece together a systematic theology of our own that aligns with our experience of the journey.

Involuntary surrender conversions are quite different and often unbelievably profound. Take for example, the experience of Doug. I met Doug in my first time in seminary in the early 70s. He had been an atheist most of his life, but he had an experience that rocked his world. Between his undergraduate and an intended graduate program in engineering, Doug spent a summer in Switzerland where he wanted to learn to be an expedition leader for mountain climbers. Each day, he and his cohort would take climbs in the high peaks of the Alps, and on weekends they had free time. Doug, however, was a determined student and wanted to build his expertise as a climber as well. So, on weekends he would go off on solo climbs, traversing glaciers and practicing his scrambling skills.

One Sunday, he was high on a glacier when he lost his footing. Instinctively, he faced downhill and, using his ice axe began what is called a glissade, a controlled slide down the ice surface. As Doug described it, a standing glissade usually becomes a sitting glissade which it did for him. He tucked the axe under his armpit and proceeded to put on the brakes, but a protruding rock quickly dashed that idea ripping the axe from his grip. He was now speeding down the surface of the glacier facing what surely would be his demise as he flew off the edge. Doug tried to recall what he had climbed over to get to the glacier and remembered the sharp granite rocks below. As he shot off the end, he knew he would die, so he had this strange thought: "if there is a God, I'm going to show him what I am made of!" So. he arched his back, closed his eyes, and put a big grin on his face, preparing to have his head crushed in the collision with the rocks.

What Doug had not figured on was that, though the rocks were directly below the cliff's edge, any snow that had landed on the glacier, would shoot off at an angle; the same angle that Doug's body took, landing him head-first in a huge mound of snow. Doug thought for a moment, "So, this is what death is like. I didn't even notice the transition from life." Doug said that when he realized what had happened and that he was in a mound of snow, he laid there giggling for a good ten minutes. "I had wanted to show this God-thing what I was made of, and instead, God had shown me what love was made of." That one experience set him on a path of discovery, and seminary was where he needed to go.

Most of us can't claim such a dramatic and pivotal moment, like Doug's, that set us on the path toward spiritual discovery. But radical conversion experiences are like that. Perhaps you have had some sort of experience where Spirit "spoke" into you, where something was awakened inside. Some report it as having seen or realized something that can no longer be "unseen." Once you are awakened by the spirit, you cannot go back to a sleep state. Others describe more slowly opening to the spiritual journey of the educational variety.

Rebecca was a bright student in high school, in fact the valedictorian of her class. And she had been brought up in a church-going family. Her mom was a Catholic and had at one time been a Third Order novitiate in the Franciscan order, intending to become a nun. Her father was a seminary dropout but continued to be a lifelong spiritual seeker. So, this family backdrop was enough to encourage her to pray about her career choice and discern what might be best for her.

Her answer came one day in a single word: "teacher." Thus, she entered college preparing to become a teacher. She liked philosophy and psychology and thought perhaps she might teach those types of subjects. But along the way she took several religion courses, and she felt a renewed energy around her faith. One day while practicing contemplative prayer (a form of meditation), Rebecca distinctly heard "preacher, not teacher!" In her high school mind, and because she was a Catholic, ministry had never been a consideration. But in that moment, all the pieces fell into place. She recalls getting chills and at the same time thinking, "How could I lead a worship service when I cannot sing or carry a tune in a bucket?" It shouldn't matter, she thought, this was her path. She chose to become a Methodist (because they had a great record of ordaining women) and went on to seminary, and ten years after her ordination, she even completed her Doctorate in Ministry. Somewhere along the way she even found her singing voice and now keeps her mike on while leading the congregants in song. But here are a few other examples:

Thomas Merton's path to faith and ministry was anything but straightforward. He spent his early years as a self-proclaimed seeker, diving into literature, philosophy, and existentialist thought, while living a life that was often reckless and indulgent.

Then, an inexplicable pull led him to explore Catholicism—not as an escape from the world but as an entry into something deeper. Even after he became a Trappist monk, he struggled with the tension between solitude and engagement. He was pulled forward again—his writing became a voice for social justice, interfaith dialogue, and contemplation in a chaotic world.

Merton's journey shows that ministry doesn't always fit into a predefined box. He was constantly drawn beyond his expectations, discovering that service can take the form of words, activism, and even silence.

Similarly, Dorothy Day never intended to become a religious figure. As a young woman in the early 20th century, she was a journalist, activist, and social radical—more familiar with political protests than church pews. She had relationships that didn't fit into traditional moral frameworks, and she initially dismissed religion as restrictive.

But something stirred in her after the birth of her daughter. A deep longing for meaning beyond political activism led her to Catholicism, despite her resistance. When she encountered Peter Maurin, a Catholic social thinker, she was pulled even further, founding the Catholic Worker Movement, living among the poor, and serving in ways she never imagined.

Day once reflected: *"We have all known the long loneliness, and we have learned that the only solution is love and that love comes with community."* She didn't choose service; it called her. Her journey was never about fitting neatly into the church's expectations but about being pulled forward into love in action.

Jean Vanier was a professor and former naval officer who had no intention of dedicating his life to working with people with disabilities. But in 1964, after visiting an institution for men with developmental disabilities, something in him shifted. Instead of walking away, he invited two men—Raphaël and Philippe—to leave the institution and live with him in a small home. This single act of companionship led to the founding of **L'Arche**, an international movement dedicated to creating inclusive communities for people with disabilities.

Vanier's life of service was not planned; it unfolded as he stepped into relationship with those whom society had forgotten. He often said: *"The fundamental question of the human heart is not 'What can I do?' but 'Do you love me?'"* His journey was one of being pulled forward—not by a grand vision, but by small, radical acts of love.

Of course, conversion experiences are just a few of the ways we each have been pulled forward on this path. Your experience does not necessarily to lead you into seminary or any career related to your spirituality. Your path is yours alone.

Journaling: Reflect on what forces in your life are pulling you forward or urging you on. Is it an internal drive or some kind of curiosity? What events seem to pull you in and which ones repel you? Try to recognize the force field of pushes and pulls around you and your belief system.

PART TWO:
A MAP FOR THE WILDERNESS

CHAPTER FIVE

In mystic states, we both become one with the Absolute and we become aware of our oneness. This is the everlasting and triumphant mystical tradition, hardly altered by differences of clime or creed.

William James, *The Varieties of Religious Experience*

The Mystic's Path

I often take the liberty of describing this path as a mystical path, and those, like you and me who are on this journey, as mystics. But that is not ego talking or bragging about our being "special." It is simply that mystics and prophets are those people who have a direct personal experience of the spiritual or of the Divine and, most important, who trust that experience as more real and more vital than anything that an organized religion, any book or philosophical point of view has taught them. Mystics break from these traditional sources because they know in their being that truth is personal, experience is personal, and meaning-making is uniquely personal. This is, above all else, a personal journey. Though we may have some common processes and challenges, part of what makes the spiritual path so difficult is that we understand that it is ours, alone.

Thus, by definition, the spiritual path, or what the sages call the unitive path, places us out "there" in the world, seemingly all alone. This can be an incredibly lonely experience, and yet, there is an urgency to it. It demands our attention. It is undeniable. And once we have had that initial encounter that spiritual spark we are somewhat like Richard Dreyfus in the movie *Close Encounters of the Third Kind*. Everywhere we turn, we see indicators and signs that keep calling us back to the core theme. It enters our dreams. We see billboards with words that others might overlook but which for us are just another "Devil's Peak" like Dreyfus saw. It is everywhere and woven into everything.

How do you know you are on this path? What are the road signs and stages or perhaps portals through which we must travel along the way? While given different names by the various sages, the mystical path or unitive path seems to have six mile-markers that define the process. For the most part, I am lifting up some of the names and descriptions from Evilyn Underhill's classic text on *Mysticism* (2009). The stages she outlined are:

- The Awakening
- Sloughing Off (Purgation)
- Initial Illumination
- The Dark Night of the Soul
- Unitive Awareness
- Return

Awakening

For most people on this path, the process begins with an event that throws them onto the path. Here, as with most of the journey of spiritual explorers and the spiritually homeless, there seems to be no common thread except that the event is earth-shaking and undeniable. This could be a death of a loved one or a divorce. It could be as severe as a war or as horrific as the senseless mass murder of children at school. But at the same time, it could be as simple as a hymn or a scripture reading that is so far out of sacredness and love that it causes one to stand up and walk out.

To be clear here, the mystical path need not be a religious one. However, the reports that people have written tend to often come from a religious perspective. Whether it is an awakening, a letting go, or even a dark night of the soul type of experience, the mystical experience is defined mostly in terms of coming to trust one's own experience. While I often speak from my perspective of having been brought up in a particular religion and having been classically trained in theology and theological research, I will do my best to apply the same stages and categories to the non-religious experiences as well.

Whatever the source is, the result is an initial insight. For my example of the militaristic nature of those hymns we sang, the awareness and the certainty I felt was that those words and the egoic pride within the hymns had nothing to do with the message of Jesus. Where was the love? Where was embracing the enemy? And most of all, where in that win-lose paradigm was the restorative justice he and the other sages spoke of? Today as we listen to the hate-filled rhetoric of the "Christian" right, who want to make the United States a "Christian" Nationalist state that rules through a fundamentalist interpretation of scripture, many of my friends and associates may feel a similar revulsion. Often, I will tell friends that I do not wish to be known as a Christian if that means what the populist interpretation has come to mean! I would rather be called a humanist despite the fact that I do my best to emulate the teachings of Jesus and follow his path of unitive consciousness.

Of course, your awakening most likely is something different. That is the nature of this journey that it is unique to each person and often not something to which others are aligned. That is what it is! What is alienating as we awaken to that truth forces us to answer the question: can I live another day/moment inside this place that has now become so alien to me?

Within the awakening is an initial "aha" moment. We may realize that we understand the scriptures differently than those around us. We may suddenly find no wisdom or sense at all in what a preacher says at the funeral of our friend, lover, or parent. We may suddenly notice that one of those closest to us, one whom we have revered or respected for years is talking nonsense or spewing hatred. And in noticing those issues and deep differences between them and our lived experience, we become aware of our own understanding. We awaken to the fact that there exists within us, within our consciousness, an understanding and a truth that *does* make sense to us. And so, like all the mystics before us, we choose to walk away and hold fast to our "truth."

Somewhere around the mid-fifth century BCE, Siddhartha Gautama, a Hindu Prince witnessed the suffering and death outside of the castle walls, and his compassion for those who suffered opened his eyes. He rejected his elite status and went out seeking enlightenment through life's suffering, understanding that suffering and death were unavoidable. Similarly, when Francis of Assisi realized the injustice of his father's business wealth, he went to the church and stripped off his fine clothes, standing naked in front of the bishop. He could no longer wear those clothes that symbolized such wealth disparity. But these are just two of the many stories of the awakening phase of the journey. You need not become a saint or "the awakened one" in order to set off on this path, but what launches your journey is, for you, just as profound an awakening.

Soughing Off / Purgation

Underhill and many other mystics call this process "purgation." It is the process of purging ourselves of any parts of the old system of beliefs that no longer fit with our current understanding. And for some it truly is purging, like Francis taking off his fine clothes. It can begin at any age. My friend John recalls being told not to ask such "embarrassing" questions of the priest. At the ripe old age of five years, he wanted to know that if Jesus died and came back to life, how did he die the second time. He wanted to know why Mary had to be made so special, and if Jesus was just like us, why were we not just like him. I would say that was pretty insightful as a kid!

Likewise, I recall asking our minister if God had hired him for this job, and if not, who did he report to who would ensure that what he was preaching every Sunday was the right stuff. My father immediately sat me down and told me not to be a wise ass. Questioning was frowned on in the Lutheran church as it was for John and his Catholic upbringing. But these were not idle questions for us. They came from a deeper sense that there was some element of truth around there, just not in the way it was being packaged.

The same can be said of other aspects of life about which we are taught an originally simplistic logic that later experiences challenge. For example, you may have been taught to respect authority and persons of authority. Then, something happens to challenge that idea, and you experience an awakening. Suddenly, you begin to distrust everything from the police to elected officials. Sloughing off those rigid categories is difficult because it challenges us to look more deeply into the person's character. We are forced to become more aware and discerning of the types of authority. If we let go of those beliefs, we think, will it all just fall into a state of anarchy? Awakening can open our eyes to some scary realities.

Once we have that awakening experience, there seems to be no turning back. We have peered behind the curtain or unplugged from the matrix. One by one, we begin to inspect and let go of beliefs that no longer fit the new understanding. However, for some, like my friend Ann, it was so intense she remembers vomiting over and over, as if her body were purging itself of some poison. She recalls that happening several times, at church camp, after a significant event at home, and last at the funeral of her beloved "Auntie." Each time, the distasteful "untruth" was exposed and sloughed off physically. Her body just could not tolerate it. Church literally made her sick !

Most often, we do not slough off these concepts and beliefs all at one time. The process of purgation varies in length from person to person. For some, it takes the form of meditation and systematically cleaning house of those beliefs that no longer belong. Some describe it as peeling the layers off an onion! Others take an academic approach, perhaps doing extensive literature search or going so far as to enroll in seminary to seek deeper understanding of the literature. Still for others, it is a life-long quest.

One by one we come to the conclusion that this tenet or that one no longer fits with our experience. What remains constant though is that once we have stepped on to this path, what is guiding us is our experience, not some philosophical assertions. For me, I likened it to shopping for clothes. One by one, I would try on some belief or philosophy to see if it fit. Sometimes, I would outgrow something that previously fit and would have to look for a replacement that did. Sometimes, I would find a belief that held true over time. However, no matter how long this distillation process is, at some point we arrive at our new understanding wherein we have cobbled together a set of beliefs that form a consistent story line. This new understanding, having made sense, subsequently requires our letting go of more old beliefs. We could not hold on to both. We are building what theologians would call a "systematic theology," a system of beliefs that hold together as one consistent structure.

Initial Illumination

Our new understanding, devoid of the parts we have jettisoned, feels sacred and holy. We sense an aliveness when viewing life's events through this new lens. We see the beauty in things and people as they are: pure and perfect in their imperfection and normalness. I recall one beautiful warm midfall day, skipping across campus at seminary (the first time I attended). I was in love with God. I had peered into what I described as the thermo-nuclear reactor of God's creative force and saw its awesome power as a sintering place of our souls. And I was certain that I had been touched by something divine that I was being purified.

Of course, like everything on this journey each person tells a different story. Mike is an alcoholic and drug user or at least he was. When he initially found AA, he was a died-in-the-wool atheist. There was no God, and he didn't need to conjecture one in order to explain the universe, the big bang, life, death, or even his alcoholism. So, when his sponsor told him that AA was a spiritual program, he almost left in disgust. His problem was alcohol, and it was ruining his life. He wanted to get help staying away from liquor so for him, his initial "god" was the group and his sponsor. And the truth was as long as he kept going to meetings and calling others, he was staying sober. There was no lightning bolt, no tumbling out of bed to his knees. There was just the hope of sobriety.

Then one evening, he was at a friend's house. The friend, though not an alcoholic, had an extensive liquor cabinet that included some of Mike's old favorites. His buddy, not knowing of Mike's recovery, offered to make him a drink. Mike said the strangest thing happened in that moment. The words, "No, thank you. I don't drink anymore" came out of his mouth. Mike says it was the most out-of-body experience he'd ever had. He had not thought the words nor rehearsed what he might say if ever offered a drink. As he tells it, though the words came from his mouth; he did not say them. "They came out, and that's the only way I have of describing what happened." In that moment, he understood what Bill Wilson had written, that "God does for us what we could not do for ourselves." Only for Mike, that God was somewhere inside of him. It was an undeniable inner awareness that the Divine lived through him, not as some fictitious external force that controlled him like a puppeteer. Mike said he suddenly felt holy and clean. It was totally foreign but at the same time totally real and entirely his.

The initial illumination is not a false illusion, but it is only our first plunge into the new reality. It is as if someone pulled back the veil on life to expose what is really happening. It is an initial unplugging from the matrix to reveal the illusion of life that we had been taught including the illusion of the

God metaphor. Of course, as children we are not capable of understanding spirituality or the Divine at such levels of complexity, so we were given a simplistic, understandable metaphor. When the metaphor is exposed by some experience of the forces of Spirit in our lives, we begin to realize the overly simplified nature of the old metaphor. Certainly, we can still use those metaphorical terms, like sky father and earth mother, but they no longer represent a reality that looks like the God of the Sistine Chapel.

We are reminded of the oft-quoted line from Corinthians:

> When I was a child I used to speak like a child, think like a child, reason like a child, but when I became a man, I put away childish things. Now we see in a mirror dimly, but then face to face; now I know only a part, but then I will know fully, just as I have been fully known.

Paul was describing the awareness he had come to after his awakening experience on the road to Damascus. This awareness didn't come instantly as some would have us believe. After he regained his sight, Saul traveled to Mt Horeb on the Sinai Peninsula, to the cave of Elijah (the place where Elijah had heard the "still, small whisper") because he was of the lineage of Elijah and felt that perhaps some truth would be found there. Saul spent three years in contemplation, codifying his new understanding, grounded in his world-rocking experience. When he emerged as Paul, he had the fundamentals that he used in founding his many churches throughout Turkey and Greece. But notice that, as you read through Galatians, Thessalonians, Corinthians and Romans, his systematics continually evolved; he continued to use and trust his experience to shape his belief system.

This illumination is like an epiphany for many of us. It serves us well because it aligns more with our understanding and experience of life. But often people report a sense that Spirit is still a power outside of themselves. We grow comfortable with this level of illumination because it works and seems to grow with us. We begin to feel an intimacy with the powers of the Spirit and an intimacy with the God of our new understanding. We feel alive and loved, cradled by this Higher Power we have found. But it only goes so far. And then, one day it falls apart.

The Dark Night Passage

In the next chapter we will do a deep dive into the nuances of the dark night passage as it is a complex and widely varied experience. The dark night of the soul plays a pivotal role in most mystics' journey as described by Underhill. Literally I have found no two people who describe it the same way, except in their use of the associated feelings. It is haunting, painful, and desolate. In the simplest terms, the dark night of the soul is a spiritual and logical impasse. No longer does the initial illumination that we had fit with or make any sense in light of our evolving experience. What is worse, is that the feelings of comfort, the sense of being loved and nurtured by the universe are gone. They simply vaporized.

There are numerous ways the sages have described the dark night passage. Theologian and Carmelite sister, Constance FitzGerald calls it an impasse— it is like a wall that offers no way around, through, over, or under (FitzGerald, 1984). We are stopped cold in our path. John of the Cross calls it a dryness and uses the metaphor of what happens to wood as it is consumed by fire: first, all the moisture is boiled out by the flame; then, the wood shrivels and turns dark before finally being overcome by the fire. The unnamed author of *The Cloud of Unknowing* (c.a. 1375) refers to it as a cloud that so fogs the mind that one is incapable of understanding or knowing (Johnston, 1996). And Thomas Merton calls it a foreboding and desolate desert.

All those things in which we once took comfort; our favorite readings, prayer and meditation, long walks in nature no longer appeal to us. In fact, they seem dry, tasteless, boring and unfounded! Even God and our thoughts about God and our relationship with the Divine seem stupid and meaningless.

Marsha (not her real name) was a rabbi of a rather large congregation. One day, when she was alone, a member of the temple came to see her in her office and proceeded to sexually assault her. As there was no one else present in the building at the time she felt cornered and helpless but made enough of a fuss that her assailant finally left, threatening to blame her. But when she spoke up to the elders and to her area leader, she was met with denial. No one believed that this person would do such a thing, and no one believed her story. Where was the Divine in all of this? Her prayers seemed unanswered, and she fell into a deep depression and lost her faith altogether. It would be years before she found her way back to her spirituality.

Carolyn Myss is a teacher of spirituality (among many other wonderful things). But after many years of teaching about the path to a fuller spiritual life, it started to sound to her just like so many words. The meaning was no longer there for her. Try as she may, she could not connect with her inner spiritual voice. I was in a small group setting with Carolyn at that time, and I marveled at her honest transparency. Carolyn told us that she tried everything she knew as techniques, things that she had taught others over the years, but nothing worked. She described getting on her elliptical machine each day and repeating "grounded, grounded, grounded" with each step, over and over, but she would never feel grounded in her spirituality. She said that her reawakening happened gradually over several months, such that she hardly noticed the change.

The precipitating event of our dark night can be anything. It could be a single traumatic event as it was for Marsha, or happen over time, like Carolyn's. There are as many precipitators as there are people experiencing the dark night, many of which will be detailed in the following chapter. But what stands out to those who have experienced it is the unraveling of logic followed by a new "purgation." As the voyager in the dark night will find, one by one they must let go of everything they once held as sacred, even their new beliefs. More specifically, they are stripped of their attachment to those elements of faith that once were comforting or life-giving. As John of the Cross describes it, they are literally burned away in the fire. In psychological terms (a vocabulary that neither the ancients nor John of the Cross had), our ego is relieved of its central place in our conscious world. It is what Eckhard Tolle called "egocide."

The dark night passage is not a singular event for most. It is a spiritual mechanism that cooks our spirituality to boil away the impurities. But we are not ever complete. Often, people experience multiple dips into the night. And sometimes, it is one long, drawn out process lasting for years. The net result of the dark night passage is deep humility. There is no cockiness, no bragging about having survived. We have arrived at a sacred place, and anything of the ego would soil that sacredness. And so, we just sit in the awareness that has come to us, knowing that few of our friends would understand, were we able to find the words to express what has happened.

Unitive Awareness

With our egos in check, and often blown up, we are free to feel what we feel without editorializing, denying, or softening. We feel the pain and loneliness of our situation. We feel the trauma of our youth, no matter how real, violent, or misunderstood it was. We are able to own it completely as our experience. And the result is embracing that pain with tenderness and compassion. We give ourselves the compassion that we had always wanted but never knew was possible. But the big aha in that moment of compassion is that we are not alone in that experience of pain. We suddenly realize that others must have experienced their own pain, their own trauma, and with that realization we become able to provide compassion to others.

Compassion is one of those emotions that first must be experienced for oneself before it can be offered to others. Without self-compassion, anything we might want to offer to others comes across as almost patronizing. How could we possibly understand the depth of their pain unless we first had acknowledged pain in ourselves? Once we know our own pain and have accepted and embraced it as ours alone, we understand that no one else could have dealt with that for us. And by extension, we realize that we cannot "do" anything for our suffering friends. Rather, compassion is the ability to sit with someone in their pain and darkness and say, "I know I cannot take that away, but I can be here with you, beside you, and I will not abandon you as you go through this."

If and when we are able to do that, the boundary between us and them dissolves. The boundary between us and the world around us dissolves with it. We see both the illusion of aloneness and the darkness of separation as the source of pain and are struck with the oneness of all things. Pain is pain—there is no more than or less than. Suffering is suffering there is no comparison. That does not imply that all suffering is equal, just that we all at some point feel pain and suffering in a way that affects us at our core and that is one very big part of what makes us human and one.

This unitive awareness, like the dark night that brought us here, is humbling. It defies description. Even now as I write these words, I am aware of how difficult it is to put words to this experience. We have lost the egoic belief that we are special and different from one another. We have seen our suffering for what it is. We have lost the distinctions of mine and yours. We understand the teaching of the Buddha that all living beings live in the same pot and share the same roots. What benefits one, benefits all; and what hurts one, hurts all. The ancient Chinese saying that "though we are different, we were born involved with each other" finally makes sense.

The unitive path, as this is called, is one that unfolds over time. Like the layers of an onion, each new experience, each layer, reveals more of this mysterious way of being. Spiritual teacher Jim Finley talks about it as a pebble falling into the abyss of the ocean. It tumbles downward until it hits a little shelf. The pebble thinks, "Oh, this is a nice place; I think I'll stay here." But before it can get too comfortable, the ocean current sweeps it away, and it falls again, only to eventually land on another little shelf. "Oh," thinks the pebble, "this is nicer; I think I'll stay here." But again and again and again, it keeps being dislodged and landing, only to fall again. This understanding of unitive consciousness is like that; we never reach the bottom of it all. We just keep seeing more. We learned through the dark night never to say "this is it," because as soon as we think we have understanding, that gets blown up and shaken loose.

The Return

It may seem to be such a long time ago that we left the safety of "knowing" that organized religion presents to us. Our travels have taken us around the world and back, whether figuratively or literally. But the message of love, compassion and oneness is not one we are permitted to keep to ourselves. So, we return home, not as a prophet or itinerant preacher, but as a witness to that love. We cannot explain where we have been nor what has been revealed on this journey. So, we remain silent at first. But people around us, our closest friends, notice something is different. Often returning sojourners are met with comments like, "You look different; did you lose weight?" or "Did you change your hair? There is something different about you." Though we feel lighter perhaps, we still see ourselves as the same old person we always were.

It is important to note that our return has a purpose; we carry a message. But we are careful not to weaponize our learning, thinking that we are somehow better. There is no better than thou or holier than thou. Those would be thoughts of the ego, and we have removed ego from the driver's seat. Ego still exists. It is part of our human consciousness, but it is no longer the force that it was. I often like to say that it sits in the back seat blurting out directions as a backseat driver, but I am able to tune it out! One of my dear friends said she finally had to throw her ego in the trunk because it wouldn't shut up! I kind of like that metaphor.

Of course, these are just metaphorical sayings. We never really get to a state of ego-less being (at least I don't think so). What is more likely the case is that the inner "I," the I that sees itself is not the guide of our conscious being. That self, as in the "myself" seen by the observing I, is the fabrication of our minds, our ego's attempt at amassing a resume of accomplishments about which it can pridefully boast. But we have been forced to leave most of that behind in the dark night.

So, what is the message we bring home on our return? It is simply that all life is sacred and that I am no different than you. Of course, we can conceptually get the meaning of those words without having gone through the dark night and unitive understanding. But after this journey, those thoughts have an entirely different taste and feel to them. Our role becomes more like a guide through the storms of life. We understand that we cannot do this for others, but we can accompany them on their trip. We can be the reassuring presence that does not abandon them in their pain—a pain that they cannot describe, but which we know. We understand that we cannot take that pain away. We just understand how alone they feel with it, and so we sit patiently reassuring them that we will never leave them. Our message is compassion and understanding.

Journaling: Acknowledge that you have been on a winding, dusty road. Take a moment to reflect on the stages of the mystic's path as you have experienced them. What was your point of awakening and what have you purged or thrown out? Did you have a big "AHA!" somewhere along this path, and if so, what was your first big awareness? We will save journaling about the dark night reflections for the next chapter.

CHAPTER SIX

When the dark night first falls, it is natural to spend some time
wondering if it is a test or a punishment for something you have done.
This is often a sly way of staying in control of the situation since the
possibility that you have caused it comes with the hope that you can put
an end to it either by passing the test or by enduring the punishment.

Barbara Brown Taylor, *Learning to Walk in the Dark*

The prospect of this wilderness is something that so appalls most
[people] that they refuse to enter upon its burning sands
and travel among its rocks.

Thomas Merton, *New Seeds of Contemplation*

Spiritual Crisis – Passage Through the Dark Night

Of all the chapters in this book, this one might be the most
detailed and lengthy. That's because the "dark night" can be tough
to explain—some people find it confusing; others see it as totally
mysterious. So, bear with me as we take a deep dive into this often-pivotal
part of the spiritual journey. A lot of what I'll share comes from my seminary
research, which leans a little toward my academic and religious roots. But let
me remind you, a spiritual crisis doesn't have to be about religion.

This kind of tailspin—what we might call a spiritual meltdown or unraveling—isn't just something for philosophers to debate. It's part of the real, lived experience of almost every seeker. Spiritual crises can show up in all kinds of ways and with varying degrees of intensity. Sometimes, it's just a nagging question we can't shake. Other times, it's something that stops us cold—a heartbreak, a loss, a cancer diagnosis, or a moment of truth that brings us to our knees. These deeply personal, often painful experiences can last a day... or stretch on for years. Even Mother Teresa, who devoted her life to faith and service, wrote that her own dark night lasted nearly 40 years.

I first encountered the concept of a "dark night of the soul" in a seminary class called "The Soul of a Leader." The professor, Dr. Margaret Benefiel, described it as a moment when all the tools and beliefs that once helped a leader guide others just stop working. I saw this firsthand when I was consulting for a pharmaceutical startup. The company hit a wall—hard—and during a team offsite, the CEO stood up, opened his jacket like he was revealing a secret, and with tears in his eyes said, "This is all I've got. Help me help you because I'm out of rabbits to pull from the hat." That was his dark night.

We can experience a dark night in a relationship, in a marriage, in a job, or even around a scientific belief that suddenly stops making sense. What defines a dark night isn't the specific issue—it's that moment when our usual ways of making sense of the world, when confronted by our current reality, no longer work. Our beliefs, our tools, the structures we've relied on fall apart. And the same goes for spiritual crisis. Back in the day, monks and mystics had the luxury of stepping away from the world to explore these things in solitude. But today? We're trying to navigate dark nights in the middle of our noisy, busy, social-media-infused lives.

The most noted guide we have for understanding the dark night is John of the Cross, a 16th-century Spanish mystic. He was a Roman Catholic priest, so a lot of his language is steeped in religious imagery. But the essence of what he describes can speak to anyone—whether you identify as religious, spiritual, agnostic, or none of the above. Essentially, the journey he describes is a universal one: the stripping away of ego, the loss of certainty, and the emptiness that often comes before our next spiritual awakening.

⚠️ Before we go deeper, I want to offer a little reframe. In our culture, we tend to associate "darkness" with danger, fear, or negativity. But what if darkness isn't bad, and light isn't always good? They're just different states—two ways of seeing. In art, for instance, when you combine all colors of light, you get white. But when you mix all pigments (like in paint), you get black. So maybe the dark night is less about the absence of light, and more about the presence of many layers—complex, rich, and hard to separate.

Who Was John of the Cross?

Since John of the Cross is going to be our guide through this chapter, allow me to introduce him. John of the Cross was a 16th-century Carmelite friar, mystic, and poet. However, he wasn't just writing about abstract ideas— he lived through his own dark night, quite literally. He was imprisoned by members of his own religious order for trying to reform it. During that time, he wrote some of his most profound reflections, including a poem called *The Dark Night of the Soul*. In fact, he didn't actually write it. Since he was being held captive and had nothing on which to write, he memorized the verses and was only able to transcribe them after his rescue. John of the Cross' poetry wasn't meant to be polished theology or step-by-step instructions—they were raw, poetic, and deeply personal. His writings[5] are considered to be among the most detailed of the texts describing the inward spiritual journey toward union with the Divine.

---

5. John of the Cross wrote throughout his life and compiled those writings into four major works: *The Dark Night of the Soul, Spiritual Canticle, Ascent of Mount Carmel* and *The Living Flame of Love*. Though *The Dark Night of the Soul* speaks directly to our topic, its poetic and elusive structure is like a commentary along the path, whereas *Ascent of Mount Carmel* is more straight-forward and instructive and provides more structure to understanding the process of entering and passing through the dark night.

But if you're looking for a map through the dark night, John of the Cross might not be your guy in the usual sense. His writing is more poetry than GPS. But what he offers is a kind of companionship for the journey, a voice that says, "Yes, I've been there, too. You're not alone."

John didn't sugarcoat the experience. The dark night, he said, is painful. It feels like abandonment—by God, by life, by friends, and even by our own inner sense of purpose. But, he points out, it's not punishment. It's a kind of purification. The soul is being emptied of its attachments, even to ideas of God, so that something deeper and truer can emerge. For John, the pathway to union with the Divine was not through striving or achievement but through surrender and release.

In modern terms, you might say the dark night is a spiritual version of what psychologists call disorientation or deconstruction. It's what happens when the scaffolding of our belief system collapses. At first, it feels like failure. Like we've lost our way. But over time, we start to realize that losing our way might be exactly what's needed to find something deeper.

If you're going through your own dark night, it might feel like:

- Nothing makes sense anymore, not even the things that used to bring comfort.

- Prayer (if you pray) feels empty or mechanical.

- You feel abandoned—by God, by the universe, by your own soul.

- You can't go back to how things were, but you don't yet know what's next.

You might feel like you're unraveling. And in some ways, you are. But it's not the unraveling of your worth or your identity—it's the unraveling of illusions. Things that were never really you or never really the "truth" are falling away.

In Christian mysticism, this isn't considered a failure of faith—it's a deeper stage of faith. It's when the soul lets go of the need to *feel* God in order to trust that God is still there. That's heavy stuff. And it's hard to live through. But there's hope woven through it. John of the Cross believed that what feels like absence is actually preparation. The soul is being made ready—not for more doctrine or belief, but for direct experience. For union. For transformation.

He warns us that this transformation does not come easily. Perhaps that is why the bulk of his writing – certainly in the *Ascent of Mount Carmel* – concerns what this isn't or what one must let go of in the pursuit of spirituality. "To enter on this road is to leave the road; or, to express it better, it is to pass on to the goal and to leave one's own way, and to enter upon that which has no Way" (John of the Cross, 2008, p. 76).

What John of the Cross described—the loss of certainty, the stripping away of illusions, the deep inner ache for something more real shows up across spiritual paths and philosophies, often under different names. In Zen Buddhism, practitioners encounter what's known as *the great doubt*—a profound questioning of everything they thought they knew. Meditation can lead not to peace but to a terrifying kind of emptiness, a disintegration of the ego's need for control or certainty. My friend Joe was going through Boddhisatva training and sat for hours in meditation. He said at one point he started sweating profusely and thought he was losing his mind. This process can feel like everything solid is dissolving—even your physical body.

In Sufi mysticism, the language is more romantic but no less intense. The soul is seen as a lover, searching for union with the Beloved—another name for the Divine. The longing, the ache, the sense of absence are not signs that something has gone wrong, but evidence that the soul is being drawn deeper into the mystery. Rumi writes in his poem *Desire*, "The lover knows only humility—he has no choice," and, further on, that the lover desires union "more than food or drink" (Barks, 1995). The pain is part of the love story.

The Hebrew scriptures also contain deep echoes of this journey. The Book of Job is perhaps the clearest example—a man of faith, stripped of everything he thought he understood, crying out to a silent God. His friends offer neat theological answers, but they ring hollow. The real turning point comes not with an explanation, but with a kind of encounter—a voice from the whirlwind that doesn't solve the mystery but honors it. But the clincher is that the voice never comes until Job gives up his righteousness and falls silent.

Additionally, people who don't claim any religious tradition know what it's like to hit a wall—to feel lost, disoriented, stripped bare. That's the dark night. And here's the twist: it's not something you can fix. There's no spiritual trick to "get through it faster." It's not about doing more or trying harder. The dark night is more like a cocoon than a crisis. You don't control the transformation; you can only surrender to it.

Even outside religious traditions, the dark night shows up. People who lose their bearings after a profound loss, a moral failure, or a radical change in perspective may find themselves in a spiritual free fall. Old frameworks collapse. Former sources of meaning seem empty. The heart aches, not just with sadness, but with a yearning for something more real, more alive. While this existential pain may share some symptoms with depression, it's not pathological. Sometimes it's a necessary passage, a liminal space between the life we've outgrown and the life that's still being born.

What unites all these expressions is the invitation to stop clinging—to certainty, to identity, to God-as-we-knew-God. The dark night requires a letting go, a dying before the rebirth. Not everyone makes it through with their faith intact. But those who do often describe something quieter, less flashy, and far more resilient: a deeper trust, a quieter love, a spaciousness where God or truth is no longer an idea but a presence.

When we first enter on to this road, most of us haven't a clue what we are doing or what lies ahead. The reason John begins the description by detailing what the dark night is not, is more a result of understanding that anything we wish to describe, such as love, cannot fit into a nice, neat box or glib definition. We have something like that dim image in a fogged mirror as Paul told the Corinthians, which no longer serves us and which must be left behind.

John's Description of the Dark Night

John of the Cross describes the dark night not as a single event or even a linear process, but as a multi-layered passage that unfolds within the seeker. At its heart, the dark night is about transformation.

To help make sense of this mysterious process, John uses a framework that distinguishes between two broad arenas of experience: the *dark night of the senses* and the *dark night of the spirit*. He further divides each of these into *active* and *passive* dimensions. While these distinctions are helpful in offering language for what might otherwise be a bewildering interior terrain, it's important to remember that these "stages" or phases are not necessarily linear or neatly separated. In real life, they often blend, loop, overlap, and resist clear categorization.

Let's begin with the dark night of the senses. This phase relates to our attachments to sensory gratification, emotional security, and even to the consolations we receive from spiritual practices. When this "night" begins, the things that once brought spiritual joy or emotional peace begin to disappear. Prayer no longer brings comfort. Community might feel disconnected. Music, rituals, or nature may lose their power to move us. Our perception of life and the world starts to shift, and what once seemed beautiful or meaningful may now feel flat or hollow. This is deeply unsettling, especially for those who have relied on these experiences as signs of spiritual connection or progress.

The *active* part of this night refers to the conscious effort we make to let go of these attachments. It involves choices, disciplines, and inner work. The *passive* part, on the other hand, is when we feel we're being taken apart by forces we can't quite name or control. This isn't something we choose; it happens to us. As John puts it, this is where the soul is being "worked on" by something greater—Spirit, Love, the Divine—though it may not feel loving at the time. It may feel like confusion, frustration, or even abandonment.

Then comes the dark night of the spirit. If the night of the senses asks us to surrender the comforts and certainties of our outer and sensual and emotional life, the night of the spirit strikes at a deeper level—our beliefs, our theology, our sense of identity and our core of sense-making. Here, we lose our spiritual footing in a more profound way. The images or ideas we held about God, about ourselves, about what is true or trustworthy—all begin to dissolve. Even our sense of being "a spiritual person" may come into question. It's not uncommon for people at this stage to feel completely disoriented, unable to pray, unable to believe, and unable to explain to anyone else what's happening. In fact, many are tempted to walk away and forget all about their spiritual journey.[6]

As with the night the senses, John describes both active and passive dimensions here, too. The active night of the spirit involves a deliberate letting go of pride, control, and attachment to being "spiritually successful." But the passive night is deeper still: it's where all our striving, all of our knowing, all of our attempts to reach God are blown up. It's where the soul is led—not by its own power, but by grace or love—into a radical unknowing, a place where all we can do is surrender (John of the Cross, 2008, p.59).

This is, of course, a gross oversimplification of the dark night, in order that we might be able to better describe all of what is going on. In actuality (or at least in my own experience and according to my read of John of the Cross), it is nothing like that. Sense and Spirit are the names of the aspects of the soul as

---

6.   There are many believers who never experience the dark night and who may pass through life with their original thoughts and beliefs intact. Likewise, there are those who encounter the dark night and actively reject it. Neither of these are bad or wrong. They are just those individual's path of faith.

described by Greek philosophy—which still influenced the thinking of most philosophers and theologians of the 16th century.

The night of the senses and the night of the spirit are so intertwined that it is hard at times to know what, or which, is happening. Though John of the Cross does at times refer to the night of the spirit as the "second night," it is only in distinguishing it from the previously described night of the senses. Other translations call the night of the spirit the "other night."[7] Sometimes, our experience of the dark night can include moments of all these elements at once. We may feel ourselves working hard to let go (active), only to be overwhelmed by something we cannot control (passive). We may sense that our ideas are being dismantled even as our emotional anchors are slipping away. But to presuppose that the night of the spirit will wait for the "green light" to begin the spiritual work or that we can, of our own will or volition cause Spirit to do anything, erroneously leads us to the believe that the two nights are or must be sequential.

I want to pause here for another word of caution. Gerard May says that the unfortunate truth about the dark night experience is that most people are aware only of John's poetic description of the active night and that few actually understand the aspects of the passive nights (May, 2004, p. 85). Again, I want to remind us of the assertion from Joseph Campbell who once quipped that the surest way to ensure that you will *not* have a spiritual experience is to have studied it beforehand. By having names and some belief about the sequence or stages of the dark night, we will automatically begin trying to match our experience to this or that stage. Theologian Barbara Brown Taylor says, "the more ideas we have about how the dark night does or does not operate, the more we will blind ourselves to what is really happening (Taylor, 2014, p. 135)."

---

7. The authoritative translation of John of the Cross is by Alison Peers. However, Gerald May and other translations such as one recently by Mirabai Starr, each read and interpret the original Spanish slightly differently.

John of the Cross informs us that we can identify the onset of the dark night of the soul by the appearance of three signs: 1) the dryness and impotence of our former spiritual practices, 2) the lack of desire for our old ways, and 3) a simple desire to love and be loved (May, 2004, 136-142).

Spiritual Dryness

One of the most common, yet most disorienting, experiences on the spiritual path is spiritual dryness. It's a feeling of emptiness or aridity that seems to come out of nowhere—when prayer, meditation, or even the practice of faith feels dry, mechanical, or empty. For those who have known a time of spiritual closeness or inspiration, this sudden absence can feel like a profound loss.

John of the Cross describes how spiritual dryness can be a part of the night of the senses (how our senses are satisfies) and the night of the spirit (where we feel the Divine presence). It is the moment when the soul feels disconnected from the familiar comforts of spiritual practices—when the words of prayer don't resonate, the rituals no longer feel alive, and the usual sources of consolation simply don't work. These ways of sensing or perceiving both our world and our spirituality no longer satisfy our hunger. It's as if God has withdrawn, and with that withdrawal, the very sense of connection we once felt seems to vanish.

This can be a deeply disorienting time. Spiritual dryness often brings up feelings of doubt, frustration, or even guilt. If you've been accustomed to feeling moved by worship or prayer, their absence can feel like a personal failure. It may even cause you to question the validity of your spiritual life or whether you've done something wrong to deserve this distance.

But here, John's wisdom is crucial: spiritual dryness is not a sign of failure. In fact, it is often a sign of spiritual growth. In his view, the dryness serves as a way of purifying the soul, teaching it to seek God not for the emotional rewards or sensory experiences, but for God's own sake. The soul is being weaned from its attachment to the feelings or benefits that come with spirituality. The soul learns to seek God beyond emotional experiences, beyond the need for spiritual rewards.

John describes this part as the way in which a log is burned in the fire. He says that the love that burns up our illusions is like the flame. Under close inspection you will notice that the flame never touches the log. Rather, the log first begins to dry up. Sap boils out of the log, and it begins to shrivel and turn black. It is then that the gasses passed off by the log combust, and the flame burns brighter.

In this way, the dryness is a kind of gift. It forces the soul to surrender its need for tangible signs of God's presence—whether those signs are emotional highs, feelings of peace, or even miraculous occurrences. Spirituality becomes less about what we get from God and more about our willingness to love God in the silence and the absence. It's a time when the soul is purified and prepared for deeper communion with the Divine.

For many, this period of dryness may be more than uncomfortable. It's often accompanied by feelings of loneliness, confusion, and a sense of being lost. You may feel as though you are walking through a desert—every step feels heavy, the sand makes each step slide back and become less effective, and there is no visible end in sight.

The dryness allows us to examine our motives and attachments. Are we practicing our spirituality for the sense of peace it brings us? Are we still in it for the feelings of closeness or comfort? If so, the dryness may be inviting us to move beyond this. It's not that those feelings are wrong or unimportant, but that we are being led to something deeper. A love that is not dependent on feeling "good" or "connected," but one that is faithful even when the heavens feel silent.

In the desert of spiritual dryness, we may discover that God is present in a new way—no longer in the form of feelings or experiences, but in the subtle, unspoken invitation to remain at peace in the silence. The dryness itself may become the place where we encounter God most intimately, not in the ways we expect, but in ways that surprise us, that deepen our understanding of love, surrender, and presence.

Lacking Desire for the Old Ways

As we move through the spiritual journey, we come to a point where the practices, beliefs, or rituals that once felt vibrant and alive may suddenly feel hollow or even irrelevant. This shift can be unsettling. It's as if a door has closed behind us, and we're left standing in an unfamiliar space, unsure of where to go next. The loss of desire for the old ways is often a sign that we are undergoing a deeper transformation.

At first, this experience, like many parts of the dark night passage, may bring a sense of confusion or even loss. We might look back on past practices—those cherished routines of prayer, meditation, or worship—and wonder why they no longer seem to nourish us as they once did. The familiar comforts of our spiritual life, whether in structured rituals, community participation, or personal devotions, are no longer capable of quenching our soul's thirst.

However, this lack of desire is not a sign that we have lost our faith or that something has gone wrong. Instead, it can be seen as part of the soul's evolution. In the process of spiritual growth, there comes a time when we must outgrow certain practices, beliefs, or ways of relating to the Divine that were once necessary for our development but have now become limiting. Just as a child eventually outgrows their toys, so, too, does the soul outgrow certain forms of spiritual nourishment.

John of the Cross speaks of this process in terms of the soul being "weaned" from its attachment to external things. The soul, in its infancy, needs spiritual practices to feel connected to the Spirit. It needs the comfort of rituals, the assurance of familiar prayers, the structure of community, and the tangible sense of Divine presence in emotional or sensory experiences. These forms are essential during the early stages of the spiritual journey. But as the soul matures, it begins to long for something deeper, something beyond the confines of ritual and structure.

We may feel like a pilgrim without a map, unsure of where we are headed. What we once depended on—whether it's the comforting structure of religious tradition or the emotional highs of spiritual experiences—no longer guide us. The soul's hunger has shifted, and it is no longer fulfilled by the old ways of relating to the Divine.

However, this lack of desire is not to be feared, nor is it a cause for guilt. It is an invitation to move beyond the external forms of spirituality and into a deeper, more intimate connection with the Divine. It is a call to enter the wilderness of the unknown, where we must trust in God's presence without the usual signs or comforts. The soul is being invited to a more direct, personal experience of the Divine, one that cannot be mediated by external structures or rituals. Of this part of the process, John writes, "While sciences can be acquired by the light of understanding, the science of faith must be acquired without the illumination of understanding." (2008).

In this place, we may begin to realize that spirituality is not about clinging to the old ways, but about growing into something new. We are being invited to seek God not through the lens of past experiences or practices but through a fresh encounter that, at each moment, requires surrender and trust. The old ways are not wrong or unimportant; they have served their purpose.

As we let go of the need for the old ways, we create space for a new depth of connection to emerge. We learn that our relationship with the Divine is not dependent on external things or specific words and processes but is rooted in an inner knowing that transcends all external forms. This is where true transformation begins—when we are no longer dependent on the comforts of the past but are willing to step into the unknown and trust in God's presence, even when we cannot feel or see it.

Paraphrasing what spiritual teacher, Dr. Barbara Holmes, said of this process, "What I was once certain of, I am no longer certain about. What few things I am still certain about, I am not certain in the way I used to be. And I am fairly certain this will continue forever."[8]

Through all of this we must be careful not to ascribe agency to the Divine; that is to say "God did this" or "God has a plan," but rather understand that the ends and the means are the same—love. If we hold fast to the belief that the Divine nature is love, then the way to the Divine is love. The desire to be loved and the attachment to being/feeling loved is the third sign. We get to a place where our ego must let go of the neediness and surrenders to the fact that the nature of everything is selfless love. Generally speaking, the bulk of the dark part of the journey through the dark night are contained in these first two parts and need to be explored a bit more.

Things that Go Bump in the Night

Welcome to the darkest part of the dark night of the soul. This is where transformation happens—not in the spotlight, but in the shadows. The pain we feel here isn't just emotional or spiritual; sometimes, it hits so deeply and physically that it can leave us unable to move. It's the moment we realize how powerless we really are—especially our ego, which has worked so hard to stay in charge.

We may cry out for relief. We may beg God—or the universe, or Love, or whoever is listening—to make it stop. And then, at some point, a quiet truth creeps in: even Jesus wasn't spared from suffering. Whether we see him as divine, human, or both, he didn't get a free pass. That realization shifts

---

8. Barbara Holmes was one of the great teachers on faculty of the Center for Action and Contemplation. This quote came from one of her last lessons at CAC.

something in us. We start to see that suffering isn't something we can dodge. No belief system, no amount of understanding, no clever theology can protect us from it.

And here's the mystery: even in the midst of our suffering—maybe especially there—we begin to understand that no pain is outside the reach of this Love. No grief, no heartbreak, no despair is too great to be held. And when Love touches suffering, something miraculous happens. It turns into compassion. Compassion for ourselves. Compassion for others. We don't just survive the suffering—we emerge with softer hearts.

Let me pause to say: this is just how I've been able to put this into words. I know it's imperfect. It's my best attempt to describe something that doesn't really fit into language. Your experience may look very different. Your metaphors, your path, your milestones may not resemble mine at all—and that's okay. That's one of the wild things about this journey: there's no one map. No right way. We're all feeling our way through the dark together.

And somewhere along the way, something gets turned upside down. We realize we've misunderstood Divine Love. It's not here to erase pain. It's here to hold us *in* the pain. Love doesn't fix us—it stays with us. Comforts us. Stands quietly by our side through every loss and every long night.

We also start to see that we're not in charge—not of the pain, not of the timeline, not of what transformation looks like. John of the Cross tells us we need to be stripped of our addictions to the things we *think* will make us whole. That includes our cravings for certainty, satisfaction, and emotional highs. It's not wrong to feel joy in being loved. But when we *need* that joy to feel okay—when our happiness depends on things going a certain way—we're clinging. And the spiritual path asks us to let go.

This doesn't mean we stop wanting to love or be loved. But it does mean our expectations have to be loosened. The idea that *we* know what kind of love we need, what it should look like, how it should show up—that all has to go. Even our most humble-sounding prayers ("If only I had a sign, if only God would just...") are often veiled attempts to control the Infinite. And this Infinite—this Mystery—can't be boxed in by our limited ideas of what would satisfy us.

What John of the Cross calls the purification of the appetites is really about burning away what no longer serves us. And then we realize something that stuns us: none of our spiritual experiences—those moments of illumination, those intimate encounters with the Divine—can be clung to. They were never meant to be souvenirs. They just pointed us toward something, but they weren't the thing itself. Spiritual teacher and psychologist, Jim Finley, says it is like looking at the lightbulb instead of looking at what the light has illuminated! We confuse the object and the subject by trying to name and objectify the source and totally miss out on what it points us to.

That doesn't mean we give up. Far from it. It just means we stop chasing the finish line—or in this case we stop chasing God. We begin to understand that the journey *is* the destination. We stop trying to find union with the Divine as if it's somewhere "out there" and start realizing it's unfolding *right here,* in the dark, in the mystery, in the messy middle. We begin to see what that light is shining on instead of trying to identify the light.

The dark night of the soul isn't some spiritual malfunction. It's not a cosmic game of hide-and-seek. It's the necessary ground of transformation. As Loder writes, "The transformational dynamic, the engine of human development, is at best a reflection of the Spirit" (Loder, 1988, 244). We begin to see ourselves as reflections of something far greater than our little selves. What's really happening is that little self—the ego—is slowly being dismantled until what's left is the big Self. The one that's been part of the whole all along. [9]

---

9. Swiss psychologist, Carl G Jung makes the distinction between what he called the little "self" which is the self the ego has constructed, and the big "SELF" which is our authentic, true self.

Ego Death – The Bottom Line

This is the part of the journey where things finally and completely fall apart—on purpose. In the language of psychology, transformation is the process of shedding what once worked to make room for something deeper, more expansive. It's like a death and a rebirth. And just like we sometimes have to unlearn old ideas to grasp something new, we also have to let go of familiar beliefs about God, about ourselves, and about how the spiritual life "should" feel.

There's a moment (or many moments) when it feels like we've lost our grip—when our faith starts unraveling, and our relationship with the Divine feels like it's slipping away. But what if this isn't failure? What if this unraveling is actually a sign of growth? A movement into something more honest, more spacious? Each trip through the dark night changes us. Each one strips away another layer of the ego, helping us move from identifying as a separate striving self to becoming something much more rooted, much more real—what some mystics call the true Self.

These dark nights don't all feel the same. Some are stormy and loud; others creep in like fog. Their intensity and texture change depending on where we are in life and how we tend to process our inner world. But no matter what form they take, they always bring us closer to something deeper.

And here's the hard truth: this is just the beginning.

John of the Cross (2008) warns that one of these signs of the dark night— losing our ability to pray in words, feeling disoriented, wanting to be alone— are not the end. They're the doorway. He says the soul begins to realize that what it thought was understanding was really still darkness. The light we thought we had turns out to be just a flicker compared to what's coming. We think we've made it through the worst—only to find we're just getting started.

John doesn't offer much comfort. Instead, he names what's happening: the loss of language, the sense of being unmoored, the pull toward solitude—these are signs that we're being invited into a deeper kind of contemplation. One that doesn't rely on thinking, words, or effort. One that asks us to surrender even the need to understand.

He writes, "The less they understand... the farther they penetrate into the night of the Spirit, through which they must pass in order to be united in a union that transcends all knowledge" (John of the Cross, 2008, p. 120). It's not about trying harder. It's about letting go, even of the idea that we need to be "doing" anything at all. The whole idea of productivity—spiritual or otherwise—gets thrown out the window.

Still, our old patterns die hard. Most of us still feel like we need to earn this transformation. We want to prove we're worthy of love, worthy of spiritual insight, worthy of God. John sees this, too. He says the soul longs to be a martyr, to suffer for God, to make some grand gesture of devotion. But he cautions us against that. The point isn't to suffer for suffering's sake. The point is to let ourselves be transformed by what we can't control.

He writes, "These manifestations of knowledge come to the soul suddenly, and independently of its own free will... the means must be humility and suffering for love with resignation as regards all reward" (John of the Cross, 2008, p. 197). In other words: stop trying to manage it. Let the Mystery do what it will. If we'd known what this path would really ask of us, maybe we'd have stayed in the safer world of black-and-white belief systems. But something in us chose this path. So, let's keep going.

This part of the journey takes time. Ego doesn't die all at once. Meaning-making doesn't collapse in a single moment. It's a slow stripping away of everything we thought made us spiritually competent. And it happens more than once. We go through it in cycles. Over and over again.

John says that unless we're fully stripped of our "appetites"—our deep hunger for certainty, satisfaction, and spiritual success—we'll keep trying to take credit for what's actually a gift. As long as we're trying to make sense of it all, we're not quite ready to let go.

But when we *do* let go, even a little, something shifts. Our faith starts to look different. It no longer needs evidence. Our hope doesn't depend on positive outcomes. And love? It no longer starts and ends with us. The ego loosens. The need to be right dissolves. And the soul begins to rest—not in answers, but in the presence of Something greater.

Not only does this not happen overnight, it's never a straight line. But if we can stay with it, even when it makes no sense, we start to see that this darkness isn't empty. It's full of graces.

To Love and Be Loved

The third and final sign of the dark night is the call to love and be loved—both by the Divine and by others. While this may seem like a simple or obvious concept, the reality of it often emerges in ways that are much deeper and more complex than we initially expect. To love and be loved is not just a matter of affection or emotional connection; it is an invitation to surrender, to transform, and to open ourselves fully to a reality that is both transcendent and immanent.

In many spiritual traditions, love is the highest calling, the very essence of our relationship with the Divine and the world around us. For those on a spiritual path, love is not just a sentiment or a feeling—it is a way of being, an active force that shapes and transforms us. Yet, even with the most genuine desire to love, many find that the journey to fully embrace love is not straightforward. It involves layers of vulnerability, surrender, and, sometimes, pain.

At first, love often feels like something we do—an action, a choice, a gift we give to others. We love through our words, our actions, and our care for others. In the early stages of spiritual life, love is often expressed in tangible ways—caring for those in need, offering support, or engaging in acts of kindness. This kind of love is often reciprocal, where we give and receive, and the flow of affection seems to bring a sense of fulfillment.

However, as we deepen in our spiritual journey, the nature of love begins to shift. In the depths of our aloneness on this journey, something begins to change. It may start as a sense of warmth deep inside. Some report waking up and having a sense of visual clarity—like the way things seem on a bright, clear spring day. Life no longer seems so much like "gloom and doom." We may begin to experience a profound sense of being loved in a way that transcends the usual forms of affection we are accustomed to. This love is not contingent on anything we do or achieve; it is a love that simply is. It is the love of the Divine, present in all things, flowing through us and around us, whether we are aware of it or not.

DANGER DEEP WATER This experience of being loved—without condition, without expectation, without any need for return—is one of the most transformative aspects of the spiritual journey. It invites us to open ourselves fully, to receive the love that is already present in our lives, even when we don't feel worthy of it or when we feel disconnected. To be loved in this way is to be held in a space of unconditional acceptance, where nothing we do or don't do can alter the depth of the love that is being offered to us. Strangely, many of us cannot tolerate (or accept) being loved unconditionally because we see our own flaws and are only able to love ourselves conditionally as a result. How could we be loved unconditionally?

In many ways, this is the love that John of the Cross speaks of in his writings. It is a love that does not rely on our feelings or actions but is grounded in a deep, unchanging truth. It is the love of God that calls us into deeper union, even when we are not consciously aware of it. This love is both tender and powerful, allowing us to encounter both the beauty and the vulnerability of being human. It is the kind of love that invites us to release our need for control, to surrender our own will, and to trust in the love that is always with us.

To love and be loved, then, is not simply about giving and receiving affection—it is about allowing ourselves to be fully seen and accepted, both by others and by the Divine. It requires vulnerability, a willingness to be open and receptive to the love that surrounds us, even when it feels uncomfortable or unfamiliar. It asks us to let go of our defenses, to allow ourselves to be transformed by love.

As we move through the spiritual journey, the call to love and be loved deepens. It challenges us to expand our understanding of love, moving beyond the confines of personal attachment or expectation to a more universal, expansive sense of love that encompasses all beings and all things. This love is not possessive, not controlling, but freeing.

In the end, to love and be loved is the essence of the spiritual journey. It is the ultimate union, the fulfillment of our deepest longing. The big "aha" that is available on the other side of the dark night is the recognition that we are never truly separate from the Divine, that love is the very fabric of existence, and that our purpose in life is to embody that love in all that we do. Whether we are loving others or receiving love, whether we are giving or receiving from the Divine, we are participating in the great mystery of love that unites us all. And all it takes is to be broken and broken open. This process is no longer about trying to figure things out. Rather, it is one that is engaged in for the pure sake of the experience, knowing that thought and descriptions at this point are no longer confined by words but can only come from the experience itself (Buckley 1979).

Summary of the Dark Night

The function of the dark Night of the Soul is two-fold. We can think of the first of these as a kind of spiritual house cleaning. As our spirituality evolves, that which we once believed or were certain of simply no longer fits our current reality. In the dark night, we have taken out the trash and rid ourselves of those old concepts. Darkness sets in where the void or absence of beliefs once lived. We become sorely aware of this hole in our being that once was a sturdy pillar, and life feels pretty unstable and precarious. Irrespective of whatever got us here, the scary reality of our perceived nothingness forms the bulk of our emotional experience of the dark night passage.

The second function of the dark night is that it forces us into a singular mindset that is capable of experiencing only the present moment. Past and future are pushed aside because of the intensity of the dark night experience here and now. There is a certain rawness and awareness that becomes present in the void that once was our belief. However uncomfortable this may be, people who have discussed their dark night experiences with me have also said that they had never felt more present than in that place. In fact, many have described a sort of nostalgia about that state after they had emerged from their dark nights. They weren't concerned about trivial everyday life issues, yet they felt that in their being totally present in the now, they were more alive and aware than ever. Learning to be fully present to the now is perhaps the best part of the dark night passage.

Rumi talks about the results of the dark night passage. "We're not afraid [anymore] of God's blade, or of being chained up, or of having our heads severed. We're burning up quickly, tasting a little hellfire as we go. You cannot imagine how little it matters to us what people say" (Barks, 2001, p. 31).

How true! Those who have not wandered into this desolate and foreboding wilderness will never understand what we have learned, as David Whyte writes in his poem *The Well of Grief*:

> Those who will not slip beneath
>   the still surface on the well of grief,
>
> turning down through its black water
>   to the place we cannot breathe,

will never know the source from which we drink,
  the secret water, cold and clear,

nor find in the darkness glimmering,
  the small round coins,
    thrown by those who wished for something else.

David Whyte, *River Flow: New & Selected Poems*. Langley, Washington: Many Rivers Press, 2007. Reprinted with permission from David Whyte and Many Rivers Company.

With each pass through the dark night, I am reminded of a phrase attributed to Oscar Wilde: "Everything will be fine in the end. So, if it is not fine yet, it is not the end."[10]

Journaling: I call this exercise "Postcards from the Field." Write a few "postcard" type descriptons of your travels through your own dark night experience(s). Then, after meditating on them write your journal entry about how you felt and what you thought on this journey. If you have endured/ survuved several dark night passages, just pick one for now. You can come back and write more later on.

---

10. Though attributed to Wilde, it was also said by John Lennon and even repeated in the movie *The Best Exotic Marigold Hotel*.

CHAPTER SEVEN

all is merely talking which isn't singing and all talking's to oneself alone,
but the very song of (as mountains feel and lovers) singing is silence

e.e. cummings

The Wordless Experience

Spirituality is an experience. Period. It is not something one studies in a book or first feels in some lecture hall. Many times, I have heard people try to explain their spiritual experience, and what most often is the case is that they have a difficult time putting words to the experience. That's because words are the enemy of experiencing the experience. Think of it this way: you have a moment of deep awe. Something has just opened in you, and you are fully engaged in that experience. But your brain wants to do its regular job of identifying things and then comparing those to its "files' of stored memories, thereby classifying it as "like this" or "similar to that" event.

In the blink of an eye, the experience gets described and identified. But these words and descriptors are not the experience; they are only symbolic or representative of the experience. And the process of naming the experience removes us from that experience. Have you ever tried to still your mind while meditating? There is this constant mental chatter that seems to never end until suddenly it becomes still. Then, without even noticing it is happening, you think, "Ah, I am meditating," and the experience is gone. In its place is the thought about the meditative experience. Spirituality may be a bit like that at times. We have the experience that is quickly followed by the thought or thoughts about that experience. It is one of the most important reasons why ego and knowing are exposed as fallacy through the dark night.

Except that is not always the case. Seekers of Spirit and seekers of the Divine frequently talk about the experience that defies words. Patrick was one of those. Though his first truly spiritual experience was induced by an ayahuasca guided session, he soon found that he could reach the same state of awareness on his own through a form of transcendental meditation. But trying to describe it to me was impossible not because I had no frame of reference for either TM or ayahuasca, but because the emotions and physical sensations had no match in my world of words.

Others also fumbled to find ways to describe the depth or intensity of their spiritual experiences. Instead, they prefer to keep it to themselves. There was no antecedent experience their minds could compare it to, just as there were not adequate words for describing it. Most refer to what it "isn't." It's not a bodily sensation, they say, but then again, it is not something that happens inside the mental realm, either. When asked where they might locate it in their body some point to their heart while others point to their solar plexus. One person I interviewed placed his hand on the back of his neck at the C6T1 area. And many others said, "all over" or that it was a totally "out-of-body experience."

There is also an additional factor that confounds us in describing this experience of the sacred. Spiritual directors often tell of the experience their journey partners have that the 20th century theologian Rudolph Otto described as both scary and alluring at the same time. This mysterious approach/avoidance experience makes us want to run and hide, but still peek around the corner, as it were, to see what that was! For me, it felt like that same morbid curiosity as before. But then again, that doesn't really capture the experience either.

Perhaps you have had an experience like this: You were hiking in the woods and came upon a scene where the sun was shining down through the trees, illuminating the path is a unique and special way. The ambiance and feeling of the moment was beautiful to the point of being almost surreal. So, you decided to take a picture. But later, when showing the picture to your friends, it seemed as though the camera had not captured the fullness of that moment. Oh, it was a pretty picture, but it was not even close to what you experienced that day.

So. how do we describe this wordless experience? Do we simply call it spiritual and leave it at that? Is it so enigmatic that it has no place in a work of literature? Perhaps we need to turn to the poets for their answer. Poets seem to be able to capture in a few words or a couple of stanzas what others would need chapters to say. Despite the paradox of using the words of poets to express some aspects of the wordless experience, their art and craft is almost in what is not said than the words themselves. They paint word pictures around the white spaces so that we are able somehow to find ourselves inside those words and spaces. Let me present a few examples.

I began this book with a quote from Rumi that described the wordless experience of oneness. Rumi says that when we are in that place of experience, "the world is too full to talk about. Ideas, language, even the phrase 'each other' doesn't make any sense." There is no "othering" to be perceived and, since all words in essence describe other things, people and experiences, we have no words that describe our sense of oneness with it all.

Likewise, the quote at the beginning of this chapter is from an e.e. cummings poem that captures the distinction between the experience and the flood of words we often use in an attempt to describe those sacred experiences. Cummings likens this experience to the beauty one feels in singing, but contends that talking and words are just so much noise. Most of us, according to cummings, just talk to hear ourselves. But singing (his name for pure experience) is holding the silence.

Mary Oliver often finds that spiritual connection in nature as well and uses that metaphor as her homage to Spirit as she does in this excerpt from her poem *The Summer Day* (Oliver, 1992). Here we hear her describe the process of just "being" in the field.

> I don't know exactly what a prayer is.
> I do know how to pay attention, how to fall down
> into the grass, how to kneel down in the grass,
> how to be idle and blessed, how to stroll through the fields,
> which is what I have been doing all day.
> Tell me, what else should I have done?
> Doesn't everything die at last, and too soon?

In his poem "The Opening of Eyes," a poem presented in the opening chapter, David Whyte describes spiritual moments as pure experience, like opening your eyes or like the story of Moses' experience of the Divine connection he felt in the presence of the burning bush.

But one of the very best expressions of the wordless experience of spirituality comes from John of the Cross. This is a translation by Mirabai Starr (2008).

> I entered into unknowing
> and remained there,
> knowing nothing.
> This place transcends all thought.
>
> I had no idea where I was,
> but when I found myself there
> (without knowing where there was)
> I suddenly understood sublime things, ineffable things.
> I will not even try to say what I felt
> as I let myself down
> into the arms of unknowing.
> This embrace transcends all thought.

I discovered the science
of perfect peace, perfect holiness!
A direct path opened
through the heart of solitude.
Speechless, I walked into the unknown.
This journey transcends all thought.

I was so intoxicated,
so totally absorbed,
so completely enraptured,
all my senses were drained of sensation
and my spirit was filled
with an understanding beyond understanding.
This awareness transcends all thought.

Whoever arrives
in the land of unknowing
frees herself of herself.
Everything she thought she knew
falls away
and her consciousness expands
to enfold the whole universe.
This circle transcends all thought.

The higher she ascends,
the less she understands.
The dark cloud
that lights up the night
reveals itself as pure mystery.
The knower rests in unknowing.
This dark light transcends all thought.

Such knowing by unknowing
is so exalted, so potent,
that there is not a thinker alive
who can grasp it with his mind.
Who can reach that high?
We can only understand by not understanding.
This wisdom transcends all thought.

It is a science so exalted,
a study so sublime,
that no human faculty can contain it.
The only way to attain it
is to plunge into the unknown.
This leap transcends all thought.

Listen:
this sacred understanding
lies in a single sip
of the Divine Essence.
Knowing by unknowing
is an act of mercy
the Beloved pours on us.
This mercy transcends all thought (pp. 71-73).

Irrespective of our inability to put words to the wordless experience itself, many folks I have talked with have not only spoke of the wordless in one way or another, but, more important, they have talked about how important, mind-blowing, raw, and real that moment or experience was. Often, they describe the wordless experience as elusive. Having once experienced it, they feel frustrated with their attempts to experience it again, but that never seems to come from their personal effort. Richard Rohr contends that it is because such experiences of the Divine are not from our doing or our merit. He refers to them as being a kind of "Divine Ambush" (Rohr & Finley, 2012).

Spirit, God, or the Divine operates on some level outside of our being and doing. We tend to refer to this quest as a journey toward unitive consciousness. That is, we begin to discover how Spirit and the Divine are found inwardly as opposed to seeking and finding them outside of ourselves not because it just dwells inside of us, but because everything is already one. As Simone Weill (1951) has said, "We don't have to look for God. We just have to change the direction of our looking." As we move along the path of our inward journey, we occasionally experience the wordless connection to what lives in and through us.

You don't make it happen; it just comes. It's somewhat like living in a household of teenagers: there is always something happening, noises, conversations, sports events, and so many practice sessions to get to and from. Dinners are no longer sit-down events, but grab-and-go moments. Yet, in the midst of this chaos and hubbub, every once in a while, a moment happens that is pure connection, tenderness, and raw honesty. You can't force them, but you wouldn't want to miss them, either. And the only way to ensure that you experience those sacred moments is to be present. The wordless experience only happens in moments of pure presence.

Like presence as a state of being, the wordless experience is just as fleeting. It is an experience of the *now* that, as soon as it is noticed, is gone. In the *now* of the wordless experience, the hairs stand up on the back of your neck, and you have goosebumps all over. Your heart feels like it will burst wide open, and maybe it does. Sitting there in the spiritual darkness, we discover a small seed. At first. it may seem insignificant, but the more we look at it the more we begin to recognize that it is the seed of the Divine. Meister Eckhardt reminds us that if we have a pear seed, it grows into a pear tree. And an acorn will undeniably grow into an oak tree. Thus, this little seed of the Divine will grow inside us into the tree called Divinity. When cared for, this seed grows within us resulting in our own Divine nature. As you gaze lovingly at this little seed (metaphorically speaking, of course), you feel a warmth emanating from the very core of your being. There is no possible way to describe what it is or what is happening just that is it happening.

Journaling Write a free verse poem (meaning it does not have to rhyme or adhere to any sort of meter) that captures your wordless experiences, What metaphors best describe those indescribable times?

PART THREE:
SUSTENANCE ON
THE JOURNEY

CHAPTER EIGHT

If the path before you is clear, you are probably on someone else's path.

C. G. Jung

The Path of Spiritual Evolution

In studying the effects of the dark night experience, narratives seem to fall into two categories: those where the evolution and transformation of the believer's spirituality changes step-by-step with each successive experience of the dark night, and those wherein the transformation is reported as a whole. Whether these latter cases have lumped together multiple experiences as one or in fact endured one long, protracted dark night is irrelevant in that both groups ultimately end up operating from what would be described as a "non-dual" consciousness. The path toward non-dual consciousness passes through several iterations along the way, which psychologists call developmental stages, and irrespective of the actual names, it is important to consider how that developmental process occurs, to identify the steppingstones on the path.

It may be helpful to think of this chapter less as a revamping of traditional stage theories and more like an observation of the wide range of how believers interact with theology, the scriptures, and their beliefs. Think of developmental stages like walking into a gigantic house of worship filled with people from every walk of life. As the minister reads the scripture for the day or begins the sermon of the day, each person in the congregation will hear those words in a unique and individual way, based not so much on the words spoken but on the operating beliefs held by the individuals in the congregation. Just as that congregation is diverse by virtue of their education and life experiences, so are individuals scattered across a diverse spectrum of operating states by virtue of their previous experiences, including encounter(s) within the dark night. Thus, I believe that it will help shed light on where the spiritual seeker is in the process if we are able to provide a better description of the language and logic resulting from various operating beliefs at each stage.

Philosopher Ken Wilbur (2007) makes a distinction between stages and states that I think is helpful in understanding the process. Wilbur says that the identifiable levels humans pass through on their developmental journey are called stages, the same as the field of psychology. But what he separates out is what he calls our operating state, or the level of development from which we consistently act. Wilbur contends that we may in fact be able to understand the principles of stages yet to be mastered but that our operating state often trails behind.

Since it is my contention that operational states are fluid and hold within them elements of preceding states or structures of meaning-making, sometimes severe or traumatic events in our lives can hurl us backward in our operational logic scheme, thus violating the linear concept of stage theory, as previously stated. For example, a person may be well advanced and operating at a high level of conscious understanding when an event like Newtown CT or personal experience of discovering a cancerous tumor can result in thoughts of "why me," trigger questions of theodicy, and call up beliefs from our more dualistic times. Stage theorists claim that such beliefs are lost in childhood despite the fact that one often encounters otherwise intelligent and thoughtful persons who still cling to dualistic and literalistic beliefs, especially in times of duress.

As is the case in human development, spiritual progression or unfolding is more a result of reacting to external pressures and unresolvable problems than an act of choice or will or as the result of the aging process. In fact, willfulness is one of those things that gets blown up early on in the dark night. Fowler (1995) contends that under pressure we seek to align ourselves with "a power sufficient enough to sustain us" and help us through such catastrophes (p. 277). His principle of recapitulation connotes that any traumatic event causes a re-evaluation of the former logic and a reshaping of that logic to conform to the newly born operating state (my term).

In discussions with ministers participating in my thesis survey, it appears more like the initial response to tragedy and trauma is not a recapitulation or review but rather a full return to the former state, and many times to fundamental dualism. For example, one respondent, discussing an incident of sexual harassment by her up-line administrator, went through a gamut of beliefs starting with feelings of being bad (*Am I bad? What did I do to deserve this?*) to dualistic questions about God (*How could a loving God allow this to happen?*). Finding those fundamental beliefs to be equally inadequate to explain the situation, the individual then "tries on" several new belief structures until one is found that can accommodate the current reality and help "make sense" of it, eventually moving us to higher and more complex logic schemas or operating states. It is therefore the pressure of the catalytic event that forces movement (in both directions: either backward to duality or toward non-duality) rather than the "claim of ultimacy" of the succeeding logic.

Seven Stages of Development

Since the research of Darwin on, we have found that homo sapiens have not evolved as a species because we *wanted* to, but rather because we must. Spiritual development is likewise a result of earlier, more simplistic levels of logic failing to hold or understand and resolve more complex life problems. It is a total collapse of the former belief structure under the weight of or necessity for dealing with one's current reality: We must find a resolution, lest we go mad! Spiritual development according to Meister Eckhart is a process of subtraction. The more dualistic a belief system (i.e., right/wrong), the more rules the system tries to create (or add on) to handle each situation, and those rules must be broken. The former logic must break down, to be removed and be replaced by a logic and ethic that can allow for these more complex issues in life, with fewer rules, while still allowing for the existence of the previously held belief. Likewise, spiritual beliefs follow a process of unlayering as they encounter dealing with greater complexities. Both Loder and Fowler blur the lines of spiritual development with those of psychological or moral development. Loder (1998) claims:

> For this level of cognitive growth to become one's own style of thinking about oneself and one's world, it is argued that one must know suffering and loss, responsibility and failure, and the grief that is an inevitable part of having made irreversible commitments of life's energy. This negative or dark side of human life is present from the beginning, but only at the middle years does it become patently plain that patterns of ego defense against this realization are gradually collapsing and giving way to the inevitable and ultimate triumph of negation that lies ahead (p. 291).

In other words, each of these stages stays with us until it is broken and no longer works or supports us, and that often doesn't happen until we have some significant miles on our life journey, or as Loder says, our middle years.

Loder seems to brush aside what we might view as precipitating events for the dark night of the soul and chalks up spiritual development as a by-product of the grief of losing one option by virtue of having chosen another or of the negativity of latent ego defenses. But here is where the dark night of the soul comes in. Because of the centrality of spiritual beliefs to the core of our being (at the soul level, or, as psychology would say it, at the level of our fundamental understanding of self), these changes are experienced as radical and often psychologically painful transformations. Stage theories too often focus on building and the refinement of logic. But the refinement of operational states is subtractive starting from a place of separateness and difference (read that as having a set of beliefs in the uniqueness of the self as distinct from all else in the universe) from the almighty and ultimately ending in a unitive place of oneness with all things including the almighty by virtue of losing all of the false distinctions created by the ego. Coming to know Spirit through the dark night of the soul or just advancing spiritually is a process of kenosis, of emptying oneself of everything, every thought, belief or supposed truth about the Divine in order to allow the incarnation of the Spirit of God within our very being.

(i) Some of the names given to the operational stages and states are taken from both *Stages of Faith* (1995) and *The Logic of the Spirit* (1998) and incorporate some of Fowler's and Loder's language. But others include references I heard in the group of people I interviewed with respect to the transformative results they experienced. Unlike Fowler's developmental model, operating states are not bound to ages or developmental stages. Additionally, we often operate at a lower state than the stages we can fully comprehend. And, developmental psychologists (like Lawrence Kohlberg, William Perry and Carol Gilligan to name a few[11]) tell us that we can usually grasp and understand only one or two stages beyond our current operating state.

1. **Dualism** – We all start learning with labels and for the most part, this labeling exists as dualities: good/bad; right/wrong; up/down and so on. Fundamentally, Western logic (and the bulk of Western theology) is dominated by the dualism of the Greeks. But even the act of labeling a table and chair carries with it the thought that by calling it a chair we are meaning also that it is not table or any other non-chair type of item. Words, by their very nature create dualism. In the conversations I've had with other seekers, this shows up as

---

11. There are of course other developmental stage theorists, but most are derived from the original ideas expressed by Erik Erikson

a kind of absolutism or certainty early in their discussion. It is a statement that "God is this" and not that. God is good, and the devil is bad. At this point, sacred scriptures are absolute truths to be taken literally as dictated by God and transcribed by human hands. For dualistic thinkers, power rests outside their grasp. Things "happen" to them. But God, they believe, has a plan, and God has ultimate power. Dualists often feel like victims if things are not going their way, and their prayer to God is a simple request to save them or to fix their current situation.

- **Power** – Dualists don't believe they have any personal power. Their only options are in reaction to powers beyond their control.

- **People** – There are two camps of people: us and them.

- **Influence** – "It is what it is, and you can't change that."

- **God** – God is almighty and "tribal," that is, "our God" cares for us, e.g., God Bless America!

- **Breakdown** – we must let go of the ideal of absolutes

2. **Questioning Seeker** – Dualism has no room in it for questions. It explains all things: God is the source of all things good; the Devil is the source of all things bad. But contrarily, once a person begins to question "reality," the absolutism of dualism has to break up. At this stage, there still exists an absolute right (God) and an absolute wrong (Devil) but there are now gradients and shades of goodness and badness. Psychologists call this state "multiplicity" for the multiple shades of gray. In the narratives I have collected over the years of studying developmental stages, some of referred to the areas of gray as confusing. Operating from the point of the Questioning Seeker allows for doubt to take center stage.

- **Power** – Questions become a sense of some power: "If I can question it, I can perhaps understand it.

- **People** – Seekers are looking more for alignment and entertain the possibility of choosing friend and foe.

- **Influence** – Choice and questioning make the Questioner the "swing" vote. "I can add my voice to define what should be."

- **God** – The Questioning Seeker says, "I know that there must be a God, but I am no longer certain what that is or what God looks like."

- **Breakdown** – We now must let go of blame and fault-finding.

3. **Committed Decider** – At some point in one's spiritual life, a distant (duality-based) God becomes personal and real one has an experience or felt perception of personal connection. At first blush, this is a feeling of being deeply and unconditionally loved. We feel touched and even called by name by God, Spirit, the Divine, or Higher Power. We begin looking at others in terms of their spiritual nature as well: "Are they one of us or not?" (Note the residual duality still living in that question?) Operating from a state of Deciding, places the Seeker in relationship with Spirit wherein decisions are no longer made by the "small self" alone but are inclusive of the soul or big SELF. And having made a commitment elements of small egoic self are lost in the context of one's purpose here.

   - **Power** – Starts shifting toward the internal. Deciders see themselves as having a say about what they are committed to doing.

- **People** – The Decider is more interactive with others, not only joining the conversation, but also seeing how to sway opinion or take in others' responses as feedback.

- **Influence** – Can convince others of their unique interpretation by virtue of their actions and follow through.

- **God** – Views God as interactive and more personal: "What would God have me do, or what would Jesus do?" Discernment becomes a more central influence in their choices and lives, not as a dictator but more like an internal compass.

- **Breakdown** – Here we lose the whole idea of accidents and start to see our ownership in everything that happens around us.

4. **Accountable** – This is where the "rubber meets the road;" where the operating state that drives a person gains traction in confronting and dealing with the issues of the world. Are you really a spiritual person? The universal law of physics which states that for every action there is an *equal* and *opposite* reaction will test one's commitments and accountability through equally powerful and "negative" or oppositional events. The very act of making a hard-and-fast commitment opens one's eyes to the barriers and obstacles that will confront or stall that commitment. The burden of carrying the weight of the world often brings the accountable person to their knees. This awareness forces us to the brink of surrendering individual effort and to falling into trusting and relying on a power greater than oneself.

- **Power** – Clarity and conviction to one's personal stand/ values becomes the source of power for actions.

- **People** – Views people as the focus of effectiveness, taking accountability not just for one's own actions but for the actions of others.

- **Influence** – Good ideas don't count unless they are received and acted on by others.

- **Spirit/God** – God is no longer seen as "out there" but rather "in here" in the soul or the spiritual feeling one possesses.

- **Breakdown** – It is a scary thought to begin to believe that you and the creator are one and that you are integrally connected to everyone else. Here is where we begin to lose our fierce independence.

5. **Conjunctive Non-Duality** – Duality finally loses its stronghold on logic and life, and the world becomes visible in terms of "both... and" (hence the term "conjunctive") understanding. What seemed paradoxical is now seen as part of a greater whole or included within the other. However, the last duality to fall is the Divine/human separation. People begin talking about the loss of meaningful boundaries, not in the negative psychopathological sense but as a sense of oneness with others and others' struggles, pains, and life situations.

   - **Power** – Clarity and conviction to one's personal stand/ values becomes the source of power for actions. The world of "possibilities" no longer exists as "probabilities" but are held as 100% possible. "I am the author of my own experience and potential."

   - **People** – Beginning to see ourselves and the Divine in others; what FitzGerald calls understanding ourselves as "we poor" and "we oppressed." Experience deep compassion for others due to seeing that they have been trapped by their own self-imposed constraints (beliefs).

- **Influence** – Beginning to see self as the source of all that one sees around them. Grounded in core beliefs and values but able to shift with each new bit of feedback.

- **The Divine** – Understanding that all concepts of god and experiences of the Divine are limited by the extent of one's personal vocabulary and experience. Therefore, God takes on a lower case as not representative of the fullness of the Divine.

- **Breakdown** – Subsequent experiences continually break down the belief in a separate God "out there."

6. **Detachment/Servitude** – As we become co-authors of our life in and through spirit, our ego and willfulness finally move aside for spiritual or divine purpose. All intellectual activity must be left behind as we realize it's downfall in trying to master things by understanding. We let go of all judgments, labels, and presuppositions and allow Divine energy to shape us. We become an instrument, a vessel, and a channel for divine purpose. Small self is no longer in the driver's seat; in fact, small self becomes only a nagging whisper in the background to which we no longer need listen.

- **Power** – Power is no longer a force of will or ego but rather comes as a result of aligning with the love of Divine nature.

- **People** – We are drawn into service where we feel most needed. We understand others' points of view, even those of our "enemies."

- **Influence** – Because of deeply understanding others' core values and views, influence comes from creating alignment through their needs.

- **The Divine** – Letting go of all preconceived notions and beliefs about god, spirit, and divinity. Understanding of Divine love living through oneself.

- **Breakdown** – Our final breakdown is in our judgements and evaluations of all things we see or encounter as good or bad, for me or against me.

7. **Universalizing** – The more we come to know God in this journey, the more we understand how little our experience has actually shown us. We stand in awe before the vastness of what we do not and cannot understand and yet which defines our very being. All knowledge is minute in relation to what is. All and anything we can be capable of knowing is finite as defined by time, place and experience, and the overwhelming realization at this point is that such experiences are just peeks and glimpses of whatever is at their source. We know without knowing while understanding that we ultimately have no clue of what it is we claim to know. We are utterly humbled by that. Yet that notwithstanding, there is a sense that this is only the beginning, that there are yet other deaths and rebirths to come.

   - **Power** – A feeling of timelessness and unbridled energy as long as we stay "on purpose," dedicated to our higher or sacred purpose.

   - **People** – Willingness to die, spiritually or physically, to protect the life of another, even if that is someone previously thought of as the enemy.

   - **Influence** – All influence is born of compassion and the ultimate care for the well-being of others.

   - **The Divine** – The Divine awareness comes with an understanding that there is a universal ethic that supersedes all temporal laws.

The bottom line in looking at any stage system is that movement is not a result of willing it to happen. Rather, like evolution itself, development only happens as a result of pressure on the previous stage until it breaks down. It is the failure or the breakdown-to-breakthrough process that moves us into each successive stage of development. We don't develop because we desire it. We develop out of necessity.

Journaling Recognizing that the difference between stages (grasping the descriptions of the various stages) and states (the level of our opersting or most frequent way of being) can be sometime quite different, write a few paragraphs about what you think you can understand stages to be and a few paragraphs on where you most frequently operate from (state).

CHAPTER NINE

There are more fake gurus and false teachers in this world than the number of stars in the visible universe. True mentors are as transparent as glass. They let the light of God pass through them.

Rumi, *The 40 Rules of Love*

Gurus, Guides and Spiritual Directors

During this journey of spirituality, it is possible to feel lost at times. Often people seek out spiritual directors or gurus to help them make sense of it all. While many people explore differing paths including meditation, education, and other formal and informal teachers, they seek some sort of spiritual authority, someone who has perhaps been down the same road or who has a form of teaching that seems to click with their lived experience. The difficulty with this is that it is not easy to find a real teacher who has experience that can assist and support the seeker on their spiritual journey.

If you were looking for a coach or trainer in some sport or for a mentor in a line of work, it would be easy to recognize them because of their results. There's an Olympic gold medal on their wall, trophies and news articles in the bookcase. At work or in professional settings, there is a long resume of results, product launches, and accomplishments. The evidence is there in plain sight. But in the realm of spirituality, it can be much harder to find the accomplished master.

Spiritual teachers can talk a good game but there is no way to prove that they have what it takes. Recall that people (ourselves included) can talk the talk of spiritual mastery, but do they walk the talk? In order for us to select a guide in this process, we will need to be observant and selective.

Gurus. Spiritual teachers, especially those who have amassed a following, are often called gurus. Guru is a Hindu word literally meaning a preceptor or intellectual providing personal spiritual instruction. The word conjures the image of a white haired and bearded Hindu monk sitting cross-legged, speaking in calm tones about life, love, and compassion. By all outward appearances, this is great. But the problem presented by many such teachers is that they often can fall under their own spell. As more and more followers surrender to their guidance, all of that power can become seductive.

Sam Harris is a neuroscientist, philosopher, and acclaimed author and podcaster. His book *Waking Up: A Guide to Spirituality Without Religion*, he details in great length how many of these self-proclaimed spiritual teachers have become abusive. He writes:

> The gurus I have met personally, as well as those whose careers and teachings I have studied at a distance, range from crooks who could be quickly dismissed to teachers who were brilliant but flawed, to those who, while still human, seemed to possess so much compassion and clarity of mind that they were nearly flawless examples of the benefits of spiritual practice. This last group is of obvious interest, and these are surely the people one hopes to meet, but the middle group can be helpful as well" (Harris, 2014, p. 168).

But it is the first group that Harris warns his readers about. These cult-like leaders have been known to require followers to perform meaningless tasks for long hours, require them to dance naked in front of an audience of strangers, or engage with the master in sexual acts with presumptive consensually. One Guru, who often raised his index finger in answer to questions, allegedly cut off the finger of one student who attempted to answer a question by doing the same! It is said that as the student, screaming in pain turned to run away, the master called him. When the student turned around, the master held up one finger, and it is said that the student was instantly enlightened. It seems like a costly lesson to me. I was once sitting in a circle of students listening to a Zen Master (not a guru) who was teaching us about presence. As I was sitting next to him, he asked me for my hand which I willingly gave to him. Without skipping a beat, he took my hand and bit it rather hard, such that I jerked it away from him. Then, he turned to me and asked, "When I bit your hand, could you think of any other thought?" I shook my head no, still rubbing the bite mark. "That is what presence is like!" These examples sound bizarre and unusual but are just small examples of what abuses can happen with teachers and gurus. Gurus too often are seduced by their own power. Harris (2014) says,

> Gurus fall at every point along the spectrum of moral wisdom. Charles Manson was a guru of sorts. Jesus, the Buddha, Muhammad, Joseph Smith, and every other patriarch and matriarch of the world's religions were as well. For our purpose, the only differences between a cult and a religion are the numbers of adherents and the degree to which they are marginalized by the rest of society... Apart from parenthood, probably no human relationship offers greater scope for benevolence or abuse than that of guru to disciple" (pp. 152-153).

He ends the chapter with the phrase *caveat emptor*. Only you can decide who is a suitable teacher for you.

There are, nonetheless, some gurus who are the exception to the above. They are neither consumed with their own power nor interested in advancing any sort of agenda. They are remarkable in their essence almost exuding or radiating love. As you approach them, they seem to want to approach you instead. You are supremely more important to them than they or their lessons might be to either of you. When they look at you, they light up as if they had just witnessed a miracle. Masterful gurus and teachers like this pull you into their world of awe and wonder. They talk of how extraordinary the ordinary is, and they lead you on a path toward your own mysticism. But I sincerely doubt that they would ever name themselves a guru. Their humility would prohibit such a thing!

When I think of this type of guru, I think of Richard Rohr, James Finley, and Cynthis Bourgeault, all from the Center for Action and Contemplation. I think of the writer/teacher Mirabai Starr and other wizened but gentle souls. I have no opinion on their suitability for you, and like Sam Harris, would say *caveat emptor* as well. Shop around. Seek them out. Sometimes, they are hiding in plain sight, disguised as ordinary, simple people.

For many years I learned from and worked with (unofficially, of course) an old gentleman who lived just down the road from me. He would not call himself a guru or a spiritual director, but he knew volumes about the natural world. At the time, I was building a post-and-beam house in northern Vermont and each day he would drive by in his beat-up Ford F-100 and give me a grade. He called me "Professor" because I worked at the local college. And he would shout out a grade for the day. "Good job, Professor. I'd give you an A today."

As a result, I would end up going to his house and sipping sassafras tea as he talked about how nature was his teacher. He learned from the seasons, from the birds and mice and hawks. Everything around him taught him. "Did you ever notice how worried mice look when you make eye contact with them?" he asked one day. "They have to be aware of everything in their surroundings all the time because they never know when that old red-tailed hawk might swoop down and have them for dinner. We might learn something about being aware and wary from those little guys."

He pointed out how Mother Nature always provided handy remedies for her more toxic plants like how jewel weed grew in the same area as poison ivy, and the juice from the pulpy stalk of the jewel weed cut the oils the ivy so it won't burn our skin. He was like my grandfather, who knew all about natural remedies. Over the several years I lived there, he taught me simplicity and respect for nature. I learned that we are only stewards of the planet, not her master. And though he would at times slip into a phrase or two in his native, French-Canadian Quebequoi dialect, he was most certainly an accidental guru. You can find them anywhere.

Spiritual Directors

Spiritual directors on the other hand provide a markedly different service to the seeker. Contrary to their name, spiritual directors do not offer advice or direction. They have been trained to be compassionate listeners who offer questions that might expand the seeker's process of deepening their spirituality. Spiritual directors accompany you on your spiritual journey as a companion, and interested listener, and a non-judgmental questioner.

Spiritual directors are often trained in many walks of theology and should not require you to belong to any particular religion or faith practice. They have received training in both the practice of spiritual direction, including coursework as well as many hours of supervision. Most spiritual directors have a director to whom they go to seek the furthering of their own spiritual quest. However, it should be noted that most spiritual directors have been schooled inside the Christian tradition. That said, it has been my experience that they do not require or even speak from their Christianity. Nor do they seem to have a particular point of view. And for this part of the journey, it is important that they not be attached to any particular religion or set of principles.

Finding a spiritual director or appropriate teacher can be a challenge. It is a highly personal process that you will have to invest some time in. In selecting a teacher or spiritual director, I would recommend interviewing several before you come to a final decision. Gurus, by virtue of their larger following, may be harder to interview in a one-on-one setting and many stories abound of gurus turning away interviewers seeking instruction (apparently that is part of the process of getting the seeker to want their instruction enough to endure the abuses)!

Selecting a Guide

Here are some questions you might want to think about before you select or interview possible guides:

- Does it matter what age they are (older, younger or the same age as you)?

- Does their gender or relationship status matter?

- Does it matter if you know them or not?

- How often do you want to meet with them? Are they open to virtual meetings as well as in person?

- What are your goals in seeking a director, teacher or spiritual mentor?

- Does it matter if they have formal training, a degree or a certificate in spiritual direction or theology?

Here are some questions you may want to consider asking a potential candidate for your spiritual guide or director:

- What is your background, your spiritual journey, your training and experience in spiritual direction?

- What in your opinion is the main purpose for spiritual direction?

- How do you define the difference between counseling and spiritual direction?

- What do you think are the biggest challenges in giving or receiving spiritual direction?

- Are there circumstances or issues that you are not comfortable discussing in spiritual direction?

- Can you tell me about a situation in which spiritual direction wasn't helpful to the person you were directing?

- Are there indicators that a person is not ready for spiritual direction?

- What do you expect of the person you are directing?

- How often do you usually meet with a person in spiritual direction?

- What is the usual length of time and format for your spiritual direction meetings?

- What questions do you have of me?

- Can you tell from our conversation what might be my biggest challenge?

Do not be too quick to judge you candidates on their credentials. A degree or certificate might not mean all that it is cracked up to be. Thus, when interviewing gurus, teachers, and spiritual directors, you might want to look for some of the following traits:

- **They are humble**. A good spiritual mentor has no pronounced ego. They are not high on themselves, nor do they talk about their credentials. Their work is not about them and their talents. It should be all about you. They will not pry but will ask opening questions about what you want and what you are currently facing on your journey of faith.

- **They are known in the community.** Most spiritual directors are well known by other leaders or retreat center directors. I sit on the Board of Directors of a retreat and conference center that not only offers training for spiritual directors but that has a vetted list of qualified directors to whom they can refer others.

- **They are compassionate.** They have suffered. Compassion comes from the personal experience of having suffered and having journeyed on this path. They know what the dark night of the soul is and what they can and cannot do in support of others going through that process. Perhaps they will not discuss their own suffering (after all, this is not about them), but you can easily tell from their compassion that they know the struggles you face.

- **They will not make decisions for you** or tell you what to do. Look for someone who will not impose their will or point of view on you. They are not there to teach or instruct. Rather they will talk about your discernment process.

- **They are spiritual.** Above all, a good spiritual guide is a spiritual person. They have a deep spirituality, a strong contemplative practice, and a habit of regular prayer or meditation/contemplation. Spirituality is not a degree or a set of accomplishments. It is a way of being.

- **They see themselves as peers.** A good spiritual director will not place him or herself in a position of authority. They often will describe themselves as a fellow seeker interested in facilitating your own journey without regard to theirs.

Of course, the above lists are only some of the basics and you should make your own set of criteria. Remember, this is a process of discernment for you. Only you and your spiritual state can determine what is right for you. Some people choose directors that they feel a deep affinity for while others seek direction from those they feel will be more challenging to work with.

Journaling What characteristics will you look for in seeking out a spiritual director, coach, or guide? If you already have a spiritual director, write out a list of their most important and valuable characteristics with respect to their ability to support your journey.

CHAPTER TEN

We are all born to fly. Instead, we sit on the branches afraid of the leap into the unknown. But the unknown is where enlightenment lives. Our true nature is the unknown.

Enza Vita, *Always Already Free*

Spiritual Emergence

I love the term "spiritual *emergence*" because it accurately describes what happens on this journey. As more and more of the layers of our egoic self are stripped away, the process allows Spirit to emerge. It emerges from within us because that is where Spirit lives inside each of us. Spirit is not only the life force beating and breathing us to life; it is the essence of the Divine with which each living creature has been imbued.

Spiritual Emergence, as it is defined in literature, is a term referring to a natural process within the realm of human development wherein individuals move beyond themselves, beyond the world as defined by mind and ego, into a transpersonal world of experience that connects them with some perception of a Higher Power, the Divine, or Spirit nature. Spiritual Emergence is an awakening that is a result of having dealt with the many challenges and difficulties in life. Through those breakdowns, one experiences something that is transcendent more stable and permanent than life and these small hiccups.

Psychologists, like Christina and Stanislav Grof, are quick to point out that if and when these breakdowns are too frequent and overwhelming, they can turn into what the Grofs call a spiritual emergency (Grof & Grof, 1989). Essentially, they see these two, spiritual emergence and spiritual emergency, on a continuum that ranges from gentle openings we can embrace to rapid, radical upheavals that transform and reshape our innermost beliefs. When the process of spiritual change becomes rapid and dramatic, this normal process may become a crisis or a spiritual emergency. Powerful feelings, images, inner experiences, and physical sensations and energies may emerge that are overwhelming and challenging to our daily functioning. When properly supported and integrated, spiritual crises can lead to deeper levels of awareness and connection to the Divine.

Spiritual emergencies can look to the untrained eye like psychotic breakdowns because of their resulting personality changes. Galena was a devout Jew all her life. She lived to help others, as she had been taught was our purpose in life. Suddenly, at the age of 79, she seemed to have cracked. She became almost ecstatically joyful and was saying things like she saw the goodness in Jesus and that there was no difference between what he taught or that which the Buddha taught and her own religion. She was dancing around with glee, hugging and kissing people, saying she could see the love of Christ in them, which really disturbed her orthodox family. They sought psychiatric help, and for a short time Galena was placed in a psychiatric hospital. While the medications they gave her calmed her, she refused to let go of her new-found insight. "You don't understand," she would say, "they are all one, *WE* are all one." The doctors classified this as a manic break, and Galena had to learn how to speak about her insight without her giddy joyfulness. Eventually she returned home and was able to hold onto her personal insight. When spiritual emergencies are understood correctly and properly supported, the Grofs say, they can result in emotional and psychological healing and drastic evolution of one's consciousness (Groff & Groff, 1989).

What I have covered thus far deals only with the process of getting to spiritual emergence. In this chapter, let's begin to consider where we are going with our emerging spirituality. Spiritual emergence, as I have said, is an awakening to this new life. It is a sort of disturbing of the waters, an upsetting of the equilibrium of the self that moves us from our daily lived level of consciousness to what might be considered a higher level of consciousness. This higher level is less concerned with self-preservation and the ego and far more focused on the world and integrating with all else. It is a process of "unselfing," if you will, where one moves from a life that was organized around one's personality and personal needs, to one that is swallowed up in the whole of the universe.

Evelyn Underhill's classification of the mystic's journey would have us believe that once we have arrived at this side of the journey, we naturally fall into a unitive consciousness. In Underhill's words, "the self slides gently, from the old universe to the new. (Underhill 2009)." But from the many conversations I have had with seekers on this path, there seem to be a number of subtle shifts in the emergent phase of their development. Let's explore each of them separately.

Healthy Doubt

There is an undeniable relationship between faith and doubt. When we were in our original faith practice (most often within the confines of an organized religion), faith was looked at as the opposite of doubt. In other words, if one truly believed X, Y or Z, then one would have no doubt. It was as if the purpose of creeds and doctrinal statements were to drive away all doubt. This certitude is, in fact, the enemy of the faith journey. Certitude stops all inquiry. It thwarts curiosity and wonder, two of the most essential elements of the spiritual journey.

Doubt, thus defined, translates into naïveté. The doubter is chastised for not believing. Christianity would cite the example of Jesus' disciple, "doubting" Thomas. But that is a misreading of the example! Thomas wasn't so much doubting but rather was bold enough to be curious and wanting to know from experience. Like all seekers, Thomas wondered and was curious to the point of boldness; something his teacher praised and then added, "Blessed are those who have not seen and yet believe"—blessed are those who have healthy doubts, wonder, and believe.

On some level there is no "real" or physical proof of God or Spirit. Of course, we can point to nature or the beauty of a sunrise or sunset as some "evidence." We can say that about the beauty and magic of birth and death or the beautiful songs of birds. And isn't Spirit present in loving and feeling loved? But these are all just subjective experiences. Even if we lean into these and so many other "spiritual" experiences, our logical minds still are left with doubt.

Doubt and faith go hand in hand. Without doubt there is no need for faith. Thus, seekers on this path have learned to supplant the doubt from their fundamental or dualistic phase with a healthy doubt that leads them to question everything to taste for themselves, to touch and feel for themselves not so that they can be certain, but so that they can experience faith held within their doubt.

Doubt is not wrong, evil, the work of the devil, or a sacrilege. It is healthy, normal, and to be expected. In fact, doubt is part of the scientific process. Scientists do not see their role as dispelling doubt, but rather to live in the space of doubt. They see their task as one of questioning facts and assumptions in a way that yields both new knowledge and further questions. A standard part of every dissertation is the section called "implications for further research." No matter how good our research had been, there is always the next question that follows from it.

But as a culture we have grown up being told we need and deserve answers. I clearly remember the rash of commercials on television (perhaps this was during the late 50s and 60s) that featured a man in a white lab coat citing the opinion of doctors and scientists as if to imply some statistical certainty of their facts. We have phrases like "prove it to me" and "says who." And, of course, there is the state of Missouri, the "Show Me" state that we somehow have elevated to sainthood! Facts and evidence rule the day, and there is no room for doubt.

Doubt may be a bit troubling to the ego, but its function is to move us toward better understanding, to questioning what is assumed or what was asserted as a proven thing by some other entity. Oh, to be certain there are universal truths and elements that are unquestionably the basis for life or structures. But in the realm of spirituality, there are no such certainties. There are no facts that stand as irrefutable. The Bible is not the infallible, inerrant word of God whose contents are somehow unquestionable or beyond reproach. It is an anthology of the stories of the early tribes of monotheism and the stories about the life and teaching of great teachers. That applies to the gospels as well. If you don't believe me, take a look at Luke 1:1-3 where the writer basically says, "so many others have told this story as they see it, it's now my turn to tell you what I have heard and gathered about these things."

So, doubt is a part of your journey. What is it that you doubt? What is it that you want to know more about? And what are the things within which you can live with doubt? The point here is that doubt is not the enemy of faith or of the spiritual quest. Doubt is not a vulnerability or weakness; it is a strength. Doubt is the seeker's superpower.

So, let's re-examine this whole doubt thing. Do you doubt the existence of a Divine being? Good for you! I am not here to say there is or is no such thing, but rather to give permission (if you need it) to question that. Digging into your doubt will help you discover just how you experience God or the Divine. You may find that there is no entity "out there" to be found. You might feel that the Divine is an in-dwelling presence or that it is love itself, the creative force of all things throughout the universe. Who knows what you might discern when you live into that doubt?

Perhaps you doubt whether you are truly a spiritual person. Then, good, dig into what that means to you. Do you doubt that Jesus was divine, the son of God or perhaps the incarnation of God as the Messiah, the anointed one? Or was he just a great prophet and teacher? I have my own opinions, but what is important is that you allow your doubt to urge you further into your discovery. As I said at the beginning of this book, spirituality is unique and individually experienced. Find yours by allowing yourself to doubt.

Voices and Visions

It is an interesting phenomenon to me that to the mystics and the ancients, hearing the "voice of God," or theophany, was a rather known and accepted experience of many seekers of spirituality. They were unashamed of their experience and generally revered for having such a direct channel of communication with the Divine. Of course, most of us are familiar with the story of the burning bush from which Moses heard the voice of God calling him into service. Some may be familiar with the symbols of the pillar of smoke or fire that led the Israelites out of Egypt. Two thousand years later Julian of Norwich received a series of 16 messages, which she called "Showings" from the Divine while lying near death in her room. These visions were so profound that she felt called back to life, and upon her recovery she spent the rest of her life analyzing the showings and then ultimately compiling them in her book, *Revelations of Divine Love*.[12]

We hear of a few modern-day mystics who have experienced theophany. Thomas Merton was standing on a street corner in Louisville Kentucky when he suddenly saw everyone around him shining with Divine light, a vision that set him on the path of discovering the interconnectedness of all beings. French philosopher, Simone Weil had a profound experience of being embraced by Divine Love, and while she never converted or joined a formal church, she

---

12. Interestingly, it is believed that Julian's book was the first published book written by a woman. The direct translation can be found in a book by Grace Warrack, but I highly recommend Mirabai Starr's book *Julian of Norwich: The Showings* (2022).

spent the rest of her life in the pursuit of justice. Of course, there are others, but it seems to us that such visions and voices happen or appear to happen less frequently today than in years gone by. If or when we do hear of it, others are quick to write it off as delusional or worse yet, psychotic.

Did Moses see a burning bush or is that just a nice story (no one was there as a witness)? Did Francis of Assisi really have the marks of crucifixion on his hands and feet? Did Anthony of Padua actually hold the infant Jesus in his arms? Did the Virgin Mary really appear and speak to the two Mexican peasants Juan Diego and Juan Bernadino? But most of all, God came as a voice heard by the prophets who then spoke for God of what God had told them to say to the people.

Though I wonder these things, I don't know. But what I do know is that those examples are spaced of a period of several thousand years. While we generally don't hear of such things anymore it may be that we just aren't paying attention or that to whom they occur and where they occur is not in our immediate circle. At one point in time, science and theology were nearly synonymous. However, with Copernicus and Galileo, the world of science was separated from its sister, theology. Religion held fast to beliefs of the anthropocentric uniqueness of this world and rejected science that pointed to other realities (the earth orbiting the sun and the solar system being just one of billions of other stars and galaxies in the cosmos). Over the ensuing 600 years, science has opened up both the understanding of our universe and of the subatomic universe. In the latter, we have discovered that what we believe to be solid is made mostly of the spaces between particles and most of what makes up outer space, rather than being void, is filled with energetic forces far greater than we imagined. In discovering these facts, science has moved closer to embracing mystery while religion has only made small strides in the direction of science. On the other hand, the human curiosity of cosmology and the origins of our world have perennially pointed us toward the stars and to thoughts of the Divine and of creative forces beyond our ability to measure.

It might seem that in days gone by, we humans lived more in wonder and question. Humans have always sensed something greater than themselves but were not able or lacked the tools to explore the outer reaches of scientific inquiry. Perhaps we wished it so hard that we willed *vox dei* into existence. Perhaps we want to hear from the Divine so badly that we actually did! We could not conceptualize of nor relate to a God that defied imagination or logic, so we needed to ascribe human characteristics to our god. We gave God a will, made God a male/father figure, and imagined "his" hands and heart to be able to hold us; really, physically. So, when we got an example of a human being, like Jesus, who had divine qualities, we made him into our God as well. Whatever the case, our need for a relatable God made Jesus the man into an avatar of the Divine. Likewise, the need for a maternal divinity expressed itself in the form of Mary, the mother of Jesus. What makes Jesus and Mary so relatable is their humanness and suffering, but what made them divine was *our* ascribing superhuman natures to them (Ehrman, 2015).

That is what the "rationalists" would say. It's all in our imagination, they would have us believe. But is it really? Is it still possible to physically experience, through our eyes and ears, the presence of the Divine? Underhill says yes, of course: "In other words, supersensual intuitions the contact between man's finite being and the Infinite Being in which it is immersed can express themselves by means of almost any kind of sensory automatism." She continues, "Strange sweet perfumes and tastes, physical sensations of touch, inward fires, are reported over and over again in connection with such spiritual adventures" (Underhill, 1911/2009, p. 193). It is a wonderful quality of human nature that does not limit experience to cognition alone. Thus, we must take them into consideration if we are to explore the realm of spiritual emergence. Further, if one were to believe in the in-dwelling Spirit as I do, it would seem logical that such an inner knowing could or would manifest through our other senses.

Our senses are simply the medium through which we perceive the world, so it only stands to reason that they would be how we might perceive the realm of the spiritual. Perhaps you (and certainly I) may not have our "burning bush" moments, but many of us on this path have had direct encounters with the Divine or with Spirit.

For many years, I had what I would consider conversations with the Divine, which I call God. I perceived it as something like a voice in the back of my head, and often I would experience this while driving alone at night. At first, I referred to it as my back seat driver. But whatever it was, it was most certainly not my voice, nor the baked-in voice of my father. It was calm and certain.

Before going further with that story, let me admit that I felt a "calling" to the ministry around the time of my graduation from high school. It was the time of the Six-Day Arab/Israeli war in June of 1967. Our church group had started a prayer vigil, and I had the overnight shift. By two a.m., I had read all the Psalms, all of the ritual prayers, and most of the hymns in the front of the hymnal. I had run out of things to occupy my thoughts and had fallen into a thoughtless silence for a moment, when I heard, as clear as day, "Lead them." That was all. The hair on my neck stood up on end. It totally spooked me. I looked around for its source but confirmed that I was alone. I had no idea what it meant or whom I was to lead. After all, I hadn't even started college. I was no leader, but that was what I heard. The next day I spoke with our pastor who suggested that it might be a calling (a totally foreign concept as well). And that was the beginning.

But what also came with the voice was a sense of some presence—something other than me, the breeze, or the silence of the church. I continued to sense the presence for many years, sometimes engaging in some form of dialogue with it. I would, for example get in my car, the hairs on the back of my neck would stand on end, and I was certain "the presence" was there again. This continued long after graduating, enrolling in seminary, dropping out, and going into another field. Until one day, 35 years later, we had it out!

Again the hairs stood up, and I snapped. "Are you still here?"

"Of course. I will never leave you."

"Look I've had it. I am tired of running away from you, from your calling, or from whatever it is you want of me. I'm done! I don't know what you want or why you would want me, but I give up. I've run out of places to hide. If you want me, you can have me: I surrender. I hereby give up control of my life. I trust and will follow whatever you want me to do."

"I'm glad you see it my way. I knew you would be ready someday."

"So, what is it you want me to do?"

"I'm sorry, that is not for you to know."

"What? This is ridiculous. I finally give in and sign up for whatever it is that you have wanted me for, and now you won't tell me what is it? Is this a game?"

"No, it's my way. You see, if I told you what I want you to do, you would try to do it and, in trying, you would try to do it your way. This is on my terms, as you just said, and done my way."

(silence)

"You gonna give me a hint?" (more silence). "Okay, then just how am I supposed to do anything? Guess?"

"Trust me. I will guide you. You will know what to do when the time comes. And if you veer off the path, I will correct you and set you back on it."

"But, but how – where do I start? What? Do I just step forward and if it is the wrong direction, you'll zap me with a lightning bolt or something?"

"Sorry, no. Wrong god! I don't work like that. I am love, that is all, and that is everything. My love will guide you. Why don't you start where you left off?"

Then, just as suddenly as it had started, it was gone. I was totally confused. Where had I even begun this quest? There was no more information and no other messages. So, I did the only thing I could think of. I enrolled in seminary the very same one I had run away from 35 years earlier. This time, I stuck it out and completed the degree program.

I'm not special, and I am not giving you this example as an exception. Rather, I share this to let those others of you who have had similar experiences know that you are not alone. Theophany still exists, and many on this path experience some version, whether it is a sense of being touched, seeing some sort of a vision or hearing words that don't come from inside your head. The question remains however, how do we know if it is real or imagined?

This requires some skill in discernment. There are several things you can do to figure out whether it's real or imagined, though none of these is foolproof. Teresa of Avila (John of the Cross' closest friend) had a quick checklist she used for discernment: Does it speak to lasting peace and clarity? Does it conform with scripture? Does it come from humility? Does it bear spiritual fruit? Does it hold some kind of enduring impact? While those might may seem to be rather hefty and difficult to determine, it can be quite helpful in the long run as you continue asking those questions. Here are but a few other techniques that I would suggest as well.

- **Lectio Divina** – Lectio is practiced a number of ways. For this effort, I might suggest that you hold the thought in mind and then open the Bible or any sacred text to any place. Let the book fall open where it will. Then, let your eyes fall on a paragraph or phrase on the page and read. The beautiful thing about sacred literature is that it is chock-full of meaning-filled statements, any one of which might apply to your current thought. Allow the text to speak to you. Often people practicing Lectio Divina will read the same passage four different times to let it speak in many ways: The first time they read the passage, they simply meditate on the text in an almost literal way. Then they read it and let the text speak into their current situation.

On the third pass, the reader reflects on the deeper meaning of the words or some part of the passage that resonate with them. On the last pass, they listen for the call to action--what does this passage and its personal meaning inspire or move them to do? Each time it is read the relevance will become clearer.

- **Prayer** – Prayer, it is said, alters the pray-er. In discerning the meaning of your theophany, your prayer is more of a contemplative prayer. That is, you want to ask your question ("what does this mean for me?"), and then sit in silence and listen. Create ample space for the still small whisper to come to you, but don't expect that it will come immediately. Let your silent listening make room for the response. Your answer may come in the form of a billboard along the highway or the simple wisdom of a child speaking to you. But don't expect thunderbolts and lightening!

- **Clearness Committee** – The Friends Society (aka Quakers) has developed a beautiful practice called the Clearness Committee. One of the best descriptions is provided by Parker Palmer. The QR code to the right will take you to Palmer's website that includes more detailed instructions. Basically, the seeker gathers a group of committed friends and first describes the situation or problem they seek clearness around. A few minutes of silence is followed while the committee formulate their questions. The committee then asks their clarifying questions, being careful not to suggest some solution by way of a question ("did you try...?"). Questions are to further the seeker's thought process. The seeker then responds to the questions as prompts to dig further into the thought process. This is followed by another period of silence. The committee then asks a series of questions that encourages the seeker to go further with their thought process again being careful not to

suggest any type of solution. The seeker writes down each question to take with them. When they are complete, the seeker acknowledges the committee for their wisdom and goes off to ponder the questions. It is a powerful process that I highly recommend.

- **Daily Walks in Nature** – Though I cannot find the source, I believe it was Meister Eckhart who said nature was the first bible (though Richard Rohr contends that it may have been the early Franciscans). Spending time in creation without electronics and the noise of traffic or machinery provides ample opportunities for insight on our message. Walking in nature you may see anything from a new sprout to a shy family of quail, a deer that stares you down, or an eagle high overhead. It is no accident that Native Americans sent out their adolescents on vision quests in nature. Nature always provided a message or a clarification for what their mission in life was to be. Whether you take daily walks or go on a formal vision quest yourself, let nature be your lectio divina practice.

Of the above, I am most partial to the Clearness Committee for two reasons. First, there is more wisdom in the collective than there is in any one individual, especially if the one is our highly subjective self. Each person on the Committee has grown up in a different environment, with different experiences shaping their meaning-making. Their objectivity is enhanced because of their separate and distinct frames of reference. How could we ever hope to have an objective view of ourselves, the way we show up to others, without input from them. We know only our intent and how we intend to show up. The Clearness Committee is a great mirror.

Second, through the Committee, we have new eyes and ears to perceive our discernment process. We are able to hear their differing perspectives on what we are saying. By tapping into the wonderment and questioning of others, each of whom may respond differently to any given choice of words or phrases we use in describing our dilemma, we are able to look at our question in ways we have never considered. Though the Clearness Committee offers no guidance, they ask for clarity (so that they might better understand what we are dealing with) and then provide us a set of challenging questions to further ponder and advance our quest for spirituality.

Journaling What is your cutting edge, or growth node that marks the place from which you will emerge spiritually? Which of the processes described in the chapter will best serve that emergence? How will you set up and utilize the process you select? If you select two or more, what to you hope to discern from each process? Get clear about your discernment goals.

CHAPTER ELEVEN

One day you will wake up and there won't be any more time to do the things you've always wanted. Do it now.

Paulo Coelho

Detachment

A big part of the spiritual journey involves letting go, or more to the point, letting go and letting come. The spiritual practice of detachment is only part of that process but a very important beginning point. Detachment involves freeing ourselves from our attachment to how things are or are supposed to be, but it does not require one to be stoic and dry.

The way detachment was described to me by a Zen Buddhist teacher (in much the same way that John of the Cross described addictions) was that he loved to hear the birds singing and there was nothing inherently wrong with that. He said he would often sit outside for his meditation time and have the birds as the background music. The singing birds lifted his spirits, and he felt happiness. But he told me, if his happiness were to be dependent on the birds singing, that would be an attachment. His happiness was a choice he made every morning irrespective of the birds singing or not. His happiness did not depend on the bird's song. Being unattached to whether the bird was singing or not allowed him to be happy by choice, and the song just added more enjoyment to this happiness.

On our spiritual journey, we come to a similar choice point. Do we believe in a power greater than ourselves or not? If that belief is dependent on evidence of that power or of its presence in our lives, we have formed an attachment about it called an expectation. If we are dependent on "answers" to our prayers, we are likewise attached to some concept of what it should be or what it might be like.

Drawing insights from Zen Buddhism, we are confronted with the notion that attachments stem from our deep-seated convictions about how the world ought to be, rather than accepting it as it is. This divergence between our conceptual frameworks and the raw, unfiltered experience of reality lays the groundwork for suffering and disillusionment.

In Zen philosophy, the concept of "beginner's mind" underscores the importance of approaching each moment with openness and curiosity, free from preconceived expectations and attachments. When we cling to rigid beliefs and expectations, we inevitably create barriers that obstruct our ability to engage authentically with the present moment. Our attachments to these mental constructs cloud our perception, obscuring the inherent beauty and complexity of reality.

Attachments extend beyond tangible possessions or interpersonal relationships; they also encompass our deeply held beliefs, identities, and sense of self. We become entangled in a web of attachments to our roles, achievements, and ideological frameworks, mistaking them for essential aspects of our being. Yet, Zen teachings urge us to peel back the layers of illusion and recognize the transient nature of these attachments.

By relinquishing our attachments to fixed concepts and embracing the fluidity of experience, we open ourselves to profound moments of insight and awakening. Zen masters speak of the liberation that arises from letting go of attachments, allowing the mind to dwell in a state of radical acceptance and equanimity. In this state of non-attachment, we cultivate a deep sense of interconnectedness with all beings and phenomena, transcending the confines of egoic separateness.

From a meaning-making perspective, the journey toward detachment is synonymous with the quest for spiritual meaning and purpose. As we release our grip on the illusion of control and surrender to the flow of life, we uncover a profound sense of liberation and authenticity. The paradox of attachment lies in its inherent impermanence; the very things we cling to are transient and ephemeral, subject to time and continual reinterpretations. By cultivating a spirit of detachment and embracing the impermanence of existence, we can transcend the confines of egoic consciousness and awaken to the boundless expanse of being. In letting go of our attachments, we discover a deeper sense of meaning and fulfillment that transcends the limitations of our mind and its meaning-making.

DANGER DEEP WATER However, let me throw in a word of caution here. Not all attachments are "bad" or in the way. We form natural attachments with those we love in several ways. A healthy attachment is the delight we have in the uniqueness of our friend or lover. Where this attachment can get dysfunctional is if we desire our loved ones to stay the way they are in our minds and never change. Then we cause suffering for ourselves as the inevitable growth happens in our friend or loved one. We have an attachment of love and caring for another person, but if we fail to acknowledge the impermanence of life, we suffer when they die. We had imagined that the person would always be there for us and that attachment only adds to the grief and suffering we feel. The amount of suffering we feel at the loss of a loved one is a direct correlate to our depth of loving that person. However, the additional suffering our ego attachment adds based in our expectations of them or our denial of the impermanence and fragility of life is what gets in the way.

Obviously, there is a lot more on this subject that you can dig into, but for the purposes of this discussion, we will leave it as some natural attachments happen and will always be a part of our experience but that we can add excess suffering by creating additional expectations meant to satisfy our egoic hunger for meaning. I particularly love how Miribai Starr treats grief and loss as absolutely normal human functions. The QR code to the right will take you to her website called Holy Lament.

How do we recognize what attachments we have? Attachments are a bit like privilege; we often cannot see the privilege from which we operate because it is so woven into the fabric of our daily lives that it is invisible. Here is a list of possible areas of attachment. You may not have attachments to all of these, but as you review the list, ask yourself how important it is in order to do what you do, in order to live the life you have, or in order to travel and function in the circles in which you live. Ask what you would be like without that status or thing. What are the words and personal characteristics you use that follow the declarations, "I am a…or I have…?" What would it mean to give those up?

Car/vehicle	House/property	Job/job title	Salary
Bank account	Accomplishments	Resume points	Net worth
Degrees	Lawn mower	Household equipment	Organizations
Church/religion	Spiritual practices	Your body image	Health/fitness
Sexual identity	Racial identity	Relationship status	Intellect
Languages spoken	Travel/places seen	Political affiliation	Opinions
Social status	Memberships	Technical skills	Social skills
Verbal skills	Family/relatives	Clothing/fashion	Music/arts
Your suffering	Past trauma	Greatest victories	(add your own)

Some of these will not apply, and others are more obvious. Be wary, however, of the ones that you immediately dismiss as not yours; those just might be attachments so ingrained that they don't appear to be attachments at all!

Use the above list as a starter list. In short, just about anything can become an attachment.

Recognizing *your* attachments is the crucial first step toward cultivating detachment. It is at first quite tricky to see, but it is only the first step in the process. There are several practices and approaches that can facilitate this process of detachment. Remember, cultivating detachment does not mean you jettison everything and disavow all connections. We are only talking about removing the psychological and spiritual weight we have attached to the importance of them for us. Here are some steps the masters list as tools of detachment:

- **Mindfulness meditation** – This involves becoming more aware of our thoughts, emotions, and sensations as they come up in the present moment. By observing attachments without becoming entangled in them, we can develop greater clarity and insight into the nature of their desires and aversions.

- **Self-inquiry and reflection** – Asking ourselves probing questions about the nature of our attachments, their source, and their underlying assumptions, we can shed light on our patterns of attachment and help loosen their grip on our experiences of the Divine.

- **Cultivating Non-attachment** – This is the core of the work we get to do. Deliberately practicing non-attachment involves consciously loosening the grip on desires and expectations. By shifting focus away from future outcomes and embracing the richness of the here and now, we can diminish the power of attachments.

- **Letting go** - Detachment often involves a process of letting go— of expectations, identities, and the need for control. This can be a gradual process that unfolds through acts of surrender and acceptance. Many folks create rituals like writing the attachment on a stone that is thrown into the lake or writing it on paper and burning it. By relinquishing the illusion of control and embracing the inherent uncertainty of life, it is possible to cultivate a deeper sense of peace and equanimity.

- **Acts of compassion and service** - Engaging in acts of service and compassion toward others can shift the focus away from ourselves and the meaning we have for various aspects of our beingness while focusing on the welfare of others. Taking ourselves out of the spotlight functionally removes the need for attachments and allows us to experience a profound sense of fulfillment that transcends our personal attachments.

From a spiritual perspective, detachment encompasses a profound shift in consciousness; a reorientation away from the egoic mind and toward the vast expanse of pure awareness. At its core, detachment involves relinquishing identification with transient phenomena and recognizing the inherent interconnectedness of all beings and phenomena. Several core constructs underpin the practice of detachment from a spiritual perspective. In essence detachment from a spiritual perspective is a journey of awakening; a journey that invites us to transcend the egoic mind, release attachment to outcomes, cultivate freedom from desire, embody equanimity and compassion, surrender to the Divine intelligence, and anchor ourselves in timeless presence and pure awareness. Through the practice of detachment, we come to a level of trust in the universe and in the Divine. However, this trust is not the former trust of our dualistic minds wherein God has a plan or God will fix this for me. We actually trust that everything is good and that all things belong just as they are.

Letting Go of Questions and Answers

Perhaps the deepest level of detachment on this journey is letting go of the need for answers and certitude. Formerly, we had been trained, by our educational systems, to seek the answer to every question. Over time we come to believe that there is a right answer for every question. Further, we were taught that it is good and right to develop a curious mind and to question everything. After all, isn't that what set us on this path to begin with? But the result of our dark night passage has been that we have started letting go of the need for answers. We learn to sit in the space of not knowing and unknowing. Eventually many of us understand that some things are beyond our comprehension. While we may come to believe in the vastness of the universe, comprehending the innumerability of stars, galaxies, planets, and whatever else is out there is a thought we can hold; the reality of it all is far beyond our limited capacity.

Ultimately, we arrive at the understanding that those questions themselves are fruitless. Our seeking to interrogate our current reality, asking what is this experience, who or what is this god, or what is the source of the universe or of what is happening all prove to be just ego's way of gaining control. Our mind believes that if it can name it and understand it, then we will have some sense of control over what seems to be totally out of reach of our control. Peace and serenity ultimately come not from understanding but from our ability to surrender to uncertainty, to embrace unknowing and mystery as the deepest level of "knowing." We come to see our need for knowing and answers as an attachment.

This journey toward detachment is deeply personal and multifaceted, requiring patience, self-awareness, and a willingness to embrace the unknown. By cultivating mindfulness, practicing self-inquiry, and embodying compassion, we can gradually release our need for attachments and awaken to a profound sense of freedom and fulfillment.

Digging beneath our attachments allows us to further understand the nature of our desires. On this spiritual journey, we gradually strip away more and more of our egoic desires for control and meaning. Understanding our desires, which so often we have perceived as needs, or worse, as essential aspects of our identity, we come to appreciate our spiritual experiences for what they really are: encounters with Divine spirit. Suddenly, we see that even our understanding of ourselves or our identities are just as manufactured as our judgments and attachments. In order to experience a full encounter with the Divine, we get to be totally, physically, psychologically, and spiritually naked. Identities like "I am a psychologist, a coach, a father, husband, son, brother (the list goes on and on)" lose meaning as each descriptor is dropped until we are left with just "I am." Stripped of all our attachments, titles, roles, accomplishments, and certainties, we come to a simple statement of existence, "I am," without any adjectives or modifiers. There, in the pureness of "I am," we can finally find connection with the great I AM of the creator/source of all.

It is both interesting and supremely funny to discover that our innermost beingness is also the source of life which we so desperately seek. The ancient writers of the Hebrew scriptures knew this when they wrote that Moses need only cite "I am" as what sent him to free the enslaved Israelites. Whether he understood that as some authoritative license to take that action or that he embraced the notion that he was (finally) enough on his own, the result was a power that was unquestionable. Personally, I believe that "I AM" was more than just telling Moses that God was sending him on the mission. For me, it was giving him (and us by extension) permission to share in the role of being source. Perhaps what the voice was telling Moses and us is that our just being is enough: I am enough. Likewise, many of us on this journey begin by looking for some blessing, someone or something that will give us permission to be. We seek validation that our own experience is enough. After all, who are we to claim that our experience is more meaningful and more valid than the great sages or some religious authority? Seemingly, the world is always questioning us, saying "Who do you think you are?" And as long as we continue to seek external validation of our roles and accomplishments, the truth of who we really are eludes us.

When we finally let go of the need for validation, that simple truth that "I am who I am" pours out of us as an ultimate truth. You are enough just as you are. You are enough to validate yourself. And most important, you are enough because you are divine. You are the Divine. The ultimate creative power that perhaps caused the universe (all universes, if you will) is what lives in you and lives in me. As the teacher Yeshu of Nazareth said it, "I am in you as you are in me and he (sic) is in me (Jn 14:20)." The life that lives us, that beats in our hearts, is the same force that has been living here since the beginning. The air we breathe and water we drink has been around and recycled again and again since the time Earth cooled from a hot mess into a life-sustaining ball. We really are a part of everything, and everything is a part of us. How validating is that?

Our egos cannot handle such a profound truth because there is no real evidence that it is the truth except for the simple fact that you are alive and breathing. And our egos need to postulate something beyond this life in order to feel important enough, as if being a part of the entire cosmos is not enough! Ego still wants status and will continue to seek it as long as we permit its arrogance to persist. That is why ego must suffer and die through the dark night passages. Often, it will take many such mini-deaths before we can accept "I am" as our reality. I do not mean to sound like the ego has a life of its own. Rather, ego is a byproduct of having a mind in the first place, and as long as we possess a brain, we will be burdened with an ego.

Letting Go as Practice Dying

As we move through this spiritual journey, we eventually discover that we must let go of self, the small self, as Jung calls it, or our egoic self as I have been using it. To the ego, that letting go feels like dying. So, before we get to our discussion of letting go, we need to dig a little into death and dying.

In life, especially here in the West, we get all kinds of training on how to win, how to compete, and how to live. Throughout my youth and the bulk of my adulthood, I was an athlete not a world-class athlete, just your regular run-of-the-mill athlete. I played sports like rugby, ran marathons, learned and competed in taekwondo, and so on. But more important, I made everything I did into a competitive sport. Even if I was throwing out a piece of paper into the waste can, I would poise like Larry Byrd and do my best free throw or maybe practice my best LeBron James three-pointer from a distance. It was sport, and I loved to score.

I was taught from an early age that in life there was winning and losing and in sports there was a score board. At the end of a game or match, the person or team with more points won, and those with lower scores went home to study and train and figure out how to do better next time. As a result, I got pretty good at winning. But no one ever taught me how to lose, I mean really sit with the pain of the loss before moving on too quickly. We never learn how to lose and let it go. It is a lesson that life is always trying to teach us: how to lose.

Then there was my divorce! There was no escaping the pain, and there was no new marriage the next week for which I could practice. There was just pain and heartbreak. It felt like dying. And that was just what it was: a little death, something I call practice in dying. I had to sit for long hours and look at my actions that led to the divorce. I had no one to blame, and even if I did try to blame her, it would not help me to deal with my pain or learn about my errors. I had to rub my nose in the pile of crap I had left on the floor like a puppy being house-trained. It was not fun. Death and dying aren't supposed to be.

But did I learn anything about letting go and about dying? I think not totally. I am still learning. So, let's start at the beginning. Life is a continuum from conception and birth through the growth and learning phases that continues to death and dying. If we do not accept death as part of the living process, we really never learn how to live. As Benedictine monk, Brother David Steindl-Rast puts it, living is a process of give and take, but most of us think of it as taking. We take a job or take a nap. We take a partner as our spouse, and so on. So, life becomes an action-oriented process that we do. But Steindl-Rast challenges us to think of how we take the action of dying when most of us think of it as something that just happens to us.

The answer is learning to let go. Each of our little deaths involve the action of letting go. We spend so much of our lives accumulating stuff (gadgets, toys, resume points, degrees, trophies, a house, a car, the list goes on ad infinitum). Spiritual teacher Richard Rohr characterizes life in two halves. The first half of life is spent building the box and accumulating stuff in the box. The second half of life should be spent giving away all of our collected gifts. The unfortunate truth, says Rohr, is that far too many of us delay the second half as long as we can and that some may never get to the second half. We have so identified with our collected things, stuff, trophies, accomplishments and roles that we think that is who we really are. And so, our loved ones are literally left with the task, both figuratively and literally, of sorting through all of what for them looks like meaningless junk or selling it off in an estate sale, never understanding or experiencing its value to us. It is only in the letting go of those things or in giving them away that people see the real value they were for us.

Thus, the process of maturation through these mini-deaths has to include learning to let go of our accumulated valued possessions. That happens one of two ways: either we intentionally learn how to let go or the letting go is forced upon us. Letting go is foisted upon us by a number of events in our life's journey. The example above of that divorce is but one such mini-death where I had to let go of my self-concept of being a nice guy, being a good husband, and so on. I had to accept the reality that I was no longer what I thought myself to be.

A different type of forced letting go occurred for me when I was running. About two-thirds of the way through my fourth Boston Marathon, my L5S1 disc exploded and tore up part of the nerve bundle that activated my lower left leg. In one instant, I went from being a runner who regularly put in 50 miles a week to never being able to run again. Oh, I can wobble, but the punishment that creates for my lower spine is not very healthy. I had to let go of the identity of myself as an athlete. So, I decided to take up other less punishing sports. I chose Taekwondo, obviously having not learned the letting-go lesson. There, over the course of the next 15 years, I rose to the level of third-degree black belt and even competed in the world championships twice. Breaking a few brittle bones in my later sixties put an end to that. Again, the message was "let go."

This time cancer became my teacher. In cancer, I finally met my match. I had to look at death as a reality, not some future hypothetical concept. I began taking stock of all the letting go lessons that had been offered to me by life. As my friend is fond of saying, "there are two types of learners in life, slow learners and people who can't learn at all. Fortunately, I am a slow learner!" I am indeed a slow learner.

I tell these stories somewhat glibly, but the truth is that life was just showing me, as it shows all who would pay attention, the impermanence of everything. One of the primary lessons in Buddhism found in *The Tibetan Book of the Dead* (Coleman, 2005) is that of impermanence. But we need not read the ancient texts to know that truth. Just walk into the forest and look at nature's lesson plan. There you will see dead and rotting trees giving life to new seedlings. You will see older trees that didn't survive the last big windstorm in their last years of life. In between, you will see growth at every stage from seedlings to fully mature giants. The entire cycle of life is right there in full display.

Now, your lessons in letting go most likely are entirely different from mine but no less significant. It may have been the death of a loved one, the loss of a business, a divorce, or any of a number of life conditions that we have come to expect as "the way it is." Sometimes, the cause of our letting go is not even something that others might consider to be earth-shaking. It may even be a minor or petty little thing that shakes you lose, like not being able to find that ring you wanted to wear one time. It could be a flat tire when you are already late for the meeting. Spirit does not care or discriminate about events like our ego does.

Each of these events, irrespective of their size and impact, that force us to let go of our beliefs, self-concepts, or attachments to our "stuff" is experienced as a mini-death, a little part of us has just died. Just as in those dark night passages these mini-deaths are practice in learning how to die because physical death, too, is a letting-go process. Physical death is just letting go of this body and this life.

As you may notice, practice in dying is not about what is on the other side of the death or mini-death. It has everything to do with how we prepare to die by letting go of attachments which must die so that when we get to that final death, we will know a bit more about how to let go of this life and this body.

Five Steps in Letting Go

As I see the process of letting go, there are five stages or steps in the process (with apologies to Elizabeth Kubler-Ross (1969) who first mapped the stages of death and dying).

8. **Denial/isolation** – The first stage of letting go might be considered step zero because it involves our unwillingness to let go. We have become accustomed to having this thing or this state, and we have formed an attachment to it. It is so much a part of our life and self-concept that we can't even conceive of not having it. As a result, we either go into hiding, putting our heads in the sand as it were, or just outright deny the inevitable. It is not so much that these things are wrong or dysfunctional but rather that they are among our normal defense mechanisms. Somehow, the primitive part of our brain doesn't want to or can't deal with the situation and mask it over.

9. **Anger/resentment** – Once we see that this death is happening, our first feeling is one of resentment. Similarly, when perhaps that aspect has been forcibly taken from us, and we have no other choice than to face it, our resistance rises to the occasion: "How could you?" "Why me?" and other such questions come from a denial of the reality of your situation. Again, this is a product of our primitive survival instinct called fight or flight. When we realize there is no escape, we will turn and fight. Though we are no longer in denial of the event, we still have not fully accepted its reality. We must first accept that reality before we can move further in the process.

10. **Depression/grieving** – Now that we have real-ized, that is we have accepted that it is, in fact real, we may be overcome by grief or depression. We finally understand that this part of our life as we know it will no longer exist. For me, it took nearly a year of grieving over the loss of muscles in my left leg before I was finally able to fully accept that reality. My self-concept as an athlete, a powerful and big man, was so elemental to my understanding of who I am that it had to come apart in pieces. Each time, I realized that there was yet another thing I could not do like I had always done before, I grieved that loss again. Often, we don't initially realize how far-reaching a particular loss is. When you lose a lover or a mate or a family member dies, there are a ton of firsts without that person with whom we had always shared. Each one is another opportunity to grieve. Grieving is an active process that we do to mark the passage of something, while depression is simply the deep sadness over the loss and its impact on us.

11. **Acceptance and letting go** – Finally, when we have grieved the loss and felt the sadness, we arrive at acceptance. The reality has set in, and there is nothing else to be done about it other than releasing it totally. Acceptance and letting go are bound together as one event.

It is only our full acceptance of the loss that marks the completion of our grief and sadness. That is not to say that we have "gotten over it," since whatever "it" was has been a part of us for so long, its phantom shadow will always remain as something we have learned to live without. At this point. we release it to the universe by letting go of our attachment to that person, thing. or aspect of ourselves.

12. **Letting come** – The final stage of the letting go process is what economist Otto Scharmer calls "letting come (Scharmer, 2007)." In the space created by letting go of the old, there is space for new awareness and new people to be let in. Letting come is a spacious openness that welcomes without prejudgment. Letting go has released our attachments and judgments and freed us to accept new realities. These next realities are neither positive nor negative. In fact, we often have let go of the need to add valences of positive and negative when we let go of those attachments.

Recently, I was at a conference led by octogenarians Fr. Richard Rohr and Dr. James Finley among others. Just a week prior to the conference one of their colleagues, Dr. Barbara Holmes, passed from this life. In a video recorded only a week prior to her death, Dr. B, as she was affectionately known, spoke about being accompanied by her ancestors at the portal. She trusted that having let go of these earthly things she now had room to clearly see her ancestors she knew were there to assist and welcome her across the portal. Likewise, Fr. Richard and "Uncle Jim" openly discussed their readiness for dying as something that brought them so clearly into focused awareness of the present moment. There was no regret, no remorse, nor any fear in any of these three elders. Instead, what we saw in each of them was a clear and present joy of living each moment.

Would that we, in our practice dying, also learn the joy of being present to each moment. Each of us, by virtue of being alive, is in the process of dying. We don't know when or how, but we all must come to the realization that we will die. Allowing that truth of our own impermanence to sink in through these mini-deaths or practice deaths is part of what has been called the wisdom path.

At my age, I have earned the right to be named an elder. But eldering is not about age. It is about having suffered "the slings and arrows" and taken the lessons from our many failures. I held a workshop once called "from ageing to sage-ing," a title I stole from a book by Schachter-Shalomi (1995). In it, I had each man take pieces of red electrician's tape and place them on a large blow up of DaVinci's Vitruvian Man to mark where his wounds were. Then, each of us described the wisdom of the wound as our rites of passage into the role of the sage.

What constitutes wisdom is the relinquishing of what we childishly cling to as important or meaningful: our accomplishments, reputation, and habitual beliefs that we are never "enough," none of which serves us. Wisdom lies in the realization that we actually have no clue what the future holds, but that we can be present to this moment. The only person who can thoughtfully and spiritually address those challenges the future may hold for us is the person we will have become in the moment we confront them. Until then, our practice and preparation for the final transition continues through these mini-deaths.

Journaling. What are you prepared to let go? Design a process or ceremony for letting each slip away Make a short list of those attachments that stand in the way of your freedom. What things are you unwilling to let go of, and why? Journal several paragraphs about the attachments you have to those things/people/habits that you still want to hold on to.

PART FOUR
HOME AND
COMMUNITY

CHAPTER TWELVE

There is a moving palace that floats in the air with
balconies and clear water flowing through, infinity everywhere,
yet contained under a single tent.

Rumi

Now Here

Mother Teresa of Calcutta once wrote in her journal, "If ever I become a saint, I will surely be one of 'darkness.' I will continually be absent from heaven—to light the light of those in darkness on earth (Kolodiejchuk, 2007, p. 230)." Though I have no delusion of ever being considered for canonization, I do identify with what Mother Teresa said. I wish to be a simple desert guide or a trail marker in the dark forest. Out here in the wilderness there is a path, your path, and I aspire to be a guide for those who wander this way. As a preteen I learned how to see the trail of an animal through the leaves and ferns on the forest floor. An untrained eye might not notice, but once one has been shown how to spot the signs, it is fairly easy to see. Whether your path leads you into the desert or a virgin forest, you can learn to see the slight signs of those who have come this way before you.

And so, we have arrived here on this path wherever that is, holding what little is left of our baggage. We have survived questions and unknowing. We have weathered dark nights, mini-deaths, and stormy times. Now, we find ourselves here with a deep sense of spirituality, a deep sense of connection to the One or to all else that is not us and yet with an understanding that we are inseparable from all of it.

But just where is "here?" Sometimes, "here" seems to look just like the place we started, the same home and family, the same neighborhood and even the same circles for friends and associates. Then there are times where "here" is as desolate as a desert or as barren as the moon. It can seem like there are no friends with whom we feel connection and no one who can understand let alone relate to our journey. Here can be a lonely place even when our physical surroundings look ostensibly the same. Then, to top it all off, there is the question of where do we go from here? How can we map out a course or direction when we aren't even certain where we are to start with?

When I began this book, I thought that there would be this great chapter at the end suggesting that there is a home somewhere for those of us who are out in the wilderness of spirituality. I fantasized that perhaps there would be a path we could all find that led us to some common ground. But alas, books tend to write themselves at some point. The author starts off headstrong with an idea of something she or he is determined to bring to the public. And then the spirit of the book or maybe even the spirit of the collection of writers now and throughout time—begins to call us forward.

Like the Lorelei, Spirit beckons us blindly forward, not to some safe harbor but to the dangerous rocks and shoals on which our clever ideas will be dashed. There she offers up her wisdom. Or maybe it is like Dr. B's ancestors saying, "Come with us."

For months, I sat with *Spiritually Homeless* mostly written but stalled. I didn't know how to take it home. Then, one day Spirit spoke. She wore the face of my dear friend Rebecca. Rebecca is an executive leadership coach, at least that is what she tells the public and anyone who would look her up on LinkedIn.

The first day we met we immediately recognized each other as fellow seekers and kindred spirits. Rebecca is a naturally charismatic spirit guide. She has been gifted with the ability to channel the Divine in the most unassuming and innocent ways. She just talks with me, but the grace of those conversations often rips me open.

"But, Kris, what if you were meant to be in the wilderness? What if that is where you were called to be so that you could write about it and help others who wander out here? What if there isn't just one path to home or even one place we call home? What if you were put here to validate others on their own very personal spiritual journeys and lead them to the home of self?"

Hard stop!

Yes, what if? The answer to that question is always that there is no "real" answer. Rather, the question of "what if?" is an opening door. We have been exploring and getting familiar with this gigantic room called our lives when finally, we bump into the wall that forms its outer edge. We follow the wall at the border of our existence until we come across that great door. "What if" is simply the key that unlocks the great door that opens into the vastness on the other side. What if we want to explore that?

Joseph Campbell, in his seminal book *Thou Art That* (2001) describes the mythic quest for the Holy Grail discussed by the Knights of the Round Table. They "thought it would be a disgrace to go forth in a group. Each entered the forest at the point that he himself had chosen, where it was darkest, and there was no way or path. No way or path! Because where there is a way or path, it is someone else's path (Campbell, 2001)." Such is the nature of exploration. There often is no beaten path to follow. There may be feint disturbances in the leaves of the forest floor or the sand crust in the desert, but those only mean that we are not alone, not that there is some "way" to follow. Of course. we can consult with our spiritual advisors, but ultimately, as we have discussed, their job is not to tell us which way to go but rather help us ask better questions so that we can discern the path ahead. And throughout this book I have described other mystics' and teachers' suggested paths. But we know in our heart of hearts that this must be our path of our own discernment.

The Road Less Traveled

I was already out of grad school and working in higher education when M. Scott Peck's book *The Road Less Traveled* (1978) came out. All my colleagues raved about it so naturally I bought a copy as well. But as I was still an arrogant young man, quite full of myself, I couldn't get past the opening page and literally tossed the book across the room in disgust. Maybe it was because already at the ripe old age of 29 I had gotten divorced, had to restart my life, and couldn't face the truth that life was indeed hard. Heck, I had moved on in life (though as I would find out later, I had not yet processed or integrated its lessons). As Peck said in that opening paragraph, "Once we truly know that life is difficult, once we truly understand and accept it, then life is no longer difficult. Because once it is accepted, the fact that life is difficult no longer matters" (p.15).

It would be years before I ever rediscovered Peck and was able to dig into his brilliant truths. Peck goes on to tell us that spiritual growth is directly linked to our self-development and specifically our self-awareness and emotional maturity. It is a road less traveled because those two personal factors require some rather difficult-to-learn skills like discipline and delayed gratification, discovering the truth of the world and acceptance of our responsibility (especially for those things we feel most affected by).

But I think the thing I learned most from *The Road Less Traveled*, that set me on this path of spiritual discovery, was confronting my fears so that I could become genuinely curious. Let me explain. At 6'3" and 220 pounds, I felt that there was nothing I feared. I played rugby on a team in Manhattan that regularly practiced on the Sheep Meadow in Central Park in the evening. It was often dark when we finished, and I would walk alone back through

Central Park to my apartment on the East Side. It wasn't a recommended practice for most folks, but I wasn't afraid!

Later, as I matured, I discovered that and the so-many-other things I did in life were done to prove to myself that I wasn't afraid when in fact I was terrified. I was afraid people would find out I was an imposter. I was afraid I was not loveable or that even I wasn't worthy of love. I was afraid I wasn't smart enough, strong enough, independent enough. So, I spent all my time trying to get smarter, stronger, fiercer, and more independent (you can read that as aloof)!

All those fears were barriers to my spiritual development. I had to confront my fear before I could ever get to the core question of who I was. If I took away all those accomplishments, titles, awards, and degrees, I feared I would be nothing. It took repeated passages through the dark nights to strip them away and show me that "I am" was sufficient. It was indeed a road less traveled. Staying conscious through the fears and the destruction of our idolatry of the ego is not something many people book as their summer vacation! But for many of us it was the road we must go down. I eventually found that copy of Peck's book and read it; in fact, I've read it several times now.

I would love to hear your story of how you got here, if only books were more of a dialogue! But I am confident that there are as many paths here as there are people who are on them. The QR code to the side of this page will take you to a site where you can share parts or all of your stories. What we have found is that hearing others' journeys often not only helps us to further understand our own but actually reassures that none of us is alone out here.

So, let's get about the business of describing where here is and what it looks like. I liked how professor and theologian Barbara Brown Taylor says it:

Once you have emerged from whatever safe religious place you have been in, recognizing that your view of the world is one worldview among many, discovering the historical Jesus, revolutionizing your understanding of scripture, and updating your theology, once you have changed the way you do church, or at least change the music at your church and hired a pastor who tweets, or you can no longer find any church within a 50 mile radius in which you can let down your guard long enough to pray, once the Dalai Lama starts making as much sense to you as the Pope or your favorite preacher and your rare but renovating encounters with the Divine reduce all your best words to dust, well, what's left for you to hold onto? After so many years of trying to cobble together a way of thinking about God that makes sense so that I can safely settle down with it, it all turns to *nada*. There is no permanently safe place to settle. I will always be at sea, steering by the stars. Yet as dark as this sounds, it provides great relief, because it now sounds truer than anything that came before (Taylor, 2014, pp. 139-140).

I agree that the first characteristic of this place is that it not only sounds true, but more important, it feels like truth if truth can be said to have a feeling. In talking with so many others who have been on this journey, there is an awesome rawness or nakedness to our spirituality. It has no frills or window dressings. It is not made up like some pig with lipstick on, as the saying goes. It is simpler than we had thought and far simpler than the doctrines and dogmas we eschewed.

Father Richard Rohr often says that if something is really true, it is true in all places across all religions and beliefs. It is that kind of truth we have been seeking and that which we may have found. The difference with this new truth is that it is ever-evolving and continually revealing its true self to us. As a result, it may not feel as settled as our former static truths had felt. We realize that the only thing that is stable is adaptability. The earth is continually changing and adapting. Our species and all species are continually evolving. We learned during the COVID pandemic that within weeks of stopping everything, the skies over Beijing cleared up, polluted rivers began to look clearer, and earth herself was reemerging as the true force of adaptability. We humans may distort things so much that we end up baking ourselves to extinction or poisoning our foods and waters enough to eradicate our species, but very quickly after our departure, the mother of us all will straighten up and dust herself off to become vital once again. Adaptability rules the day.

Shedding our skin

The paradox of the mystical path is that it is the rawness and vulnerability we feel makes it at the same time both inviting and scary as hell (used intentionally). People have characterized it to me as feeling like they were walking around outside totally naked. It's like that recurring dream many people experience of discovering you have no clothes on in a very public area. And yet, despite that awkward feeling, it feels more real and authentic than any other way of being we have ever embodied. No wonder that this is not a well-traveled road! Each time we slough off that which is not our authentic self, life gets more real and clear. And each time we adapt to our new uncomfortable nakedness, our eyes are eventually opened to a next reality.

And so, the cycle goes on and on. Sloughing off our old skin brings a new rawness, which in turn becomes the old skin that eventually must also be shed. It is what Meister Eckhart called growth by subtraction. You would think that we would become comfortable with this discomfort, but it never happens. There are those I have talked with who said that they wished the process would stop or that they could get off the train, but they never do.

One friend said it was an awareness he had that the old wineskin would eventually burst, and so he felt compelled to stay on the path lest he burst open and lose everything he had gained even though he later confessed that even that was an illusion that he had somehow gained it. It never is ours to possess. We come back to what Dr Barbara Holmes said shortly before her passing, "What I used to be so certain about, I am no longer certain about, and those things I remained certain about, I was not certain in the same way as I once was. And," she added with a smile, "I'm pretty certain this will continue for as long as I live. (personal communication, CAC Conference, November 2, 2024)"

Awareness on the unitive path toward oneness is not the same as those insights and awarenesses we had when in college and graduate school. It is more ethereal and slippery. Yes, they are thoughts and insights of sorts, but they are no longer the kind our ego desired or could "own."

Journaling. Where is "here" for you? Write about what elusive feelings you have in those moments of "now here." What was it that you wanted to hold onto so desperately? What was it like to notice how tenuous and fleeting it was? Think and write about what you can or might be able to do to bring yourself back to those open spaces and moments of clarity in the present tense.

CHAPTER THIRTEEN

As mystical awareness unfolds, the default self dissolves – a shift to self-awareness that William James called "surrender."

Dacher Keltner, *Awe*

Finding Spirit

Throughout this book, I have repeatedly used the terms *awe* and *wonder* without ever delving much into them or fully defining them. But once we are on our own, we need to look at the ways we reconstruct our story of spirituality. Freed from the past and freed from the doctrines of the world that formed us, whether those doctrines came from religious organizations or from the beliefs embedded in our host society, we now get to come to terms with our own definitions and sources of spirituality.

Given that quest, I still contend that it is our innate curiosity about that which is greater than ourselves that pulls us as seekers and explorers into this uncharted territory. While we explore, certain things catch our eye. Like the ancients Brian Swimme described, we look up at the stars and ask questions. Some things stop us in our tracks while other things simply take our breath away. It is those later ones that are awe-inspiring and that form, at least for me, the basis of my questions and for my reconstructed spirituality.

The questions seekers ask are often a result of that which appears in front of them on this path, those things that disrupt our thinking and challenge our belief that this is just another ordinary moment. Dacher Keltner describes eight different sources of awe in his book by that name (Keltner, 2023). Keltner says our experience of awe is what spurs these existential questions: when we encounter beauty in nature or in moral action, when we are swept up in the energy of the collective, are in the presence of great music or art or at the sacred places where those are found, and even at the moment of the death of a loved one. These epiphanies and experiences point to something greater than ourselves and set our minds to wondering. What inspired that? What could have created such magnificence, such beauty? I won't try to distill or repeat Keltner's wisdom but rather recommend this as essential reading for fellow seekers and explorers. However, several of his categories warrant mentioning within this discussion as I see it.

1. Moral Beauty – There are times when we are blessed to witness some act of kindness or beautiful exchange between two or more people. It is something that Keltner calls "moral beauty," and each time I have seen one of these moments I have been either silenced or moved to tears. They are indeed beautiful moments that live on as vivid memories. That moment can be a hotly contested race when one competitor seizes up and her rival stops, ducks under her arm, and tenderly helps her finish that last half mile. Or that moment can be like the time I was riding the New York City subway when a group of children got on. They had been to the zoo in Central Park and were exuberant with joy, but because the car was crowded with afternoon commuters (most of whom were reading the paper or gazing off blankly at nothing), the kids settled in wherever they could. Then, they immediately started sharing their excitement about the Polar bear or a squirrel—whatever was their highlight at the moment—with the tired commuters next to them. For the next

four stops, the entire car was transformed, buzzing with love and joy: old men talking with children, elderly women in babushkas gasping with delight as the children regaled them with their stories, formally dressed businessmen squatting down to listen to what the two kids beside him were telling!

2. Collective effervescence – This form of awe is the process of connecting with others as pure energy/spirit. The best example I have is on race day for the Boston Marathon. The streets of Hopkinton, MA are cordoned off into "corrals" of racers—the elite runners up front and the rest of the masses, between 20,000 to 30,000 runners, in the corrals behind them. If you can, imagine the feeling of 30,000 people all looking to the east, all prepared to do this outrageous feat, and all of them with just one thought and goal in mind—to make it to Boylston Street in Boston. The feeling is more than palpable; you literally feel your body vibrating or buzzing with the collective energy. Collective effervescence can be like the high you experience at a great concert or rock show, at a rave, or like when 70,000 Taylor Swift fans all sing her song in unison.

3. Wild awe – Perhaps my favorite category of Keltner's categories is the awe we find in nature. You don't have to go to Yosemite or the Grand Canyon to be inspired by the beauty and power of nature. Sometimes, it hits you in a simple woods-walk near your home. Wild awe comes in so many forms: the springtime chorus of birds all showing off their best mating calls, watching a hawk catch a thermal and spiral effortlessly upward in the sky, watching a sunset at the beach (or catching a sunrise from a mountain perch). The list is nearly infinite. Nature is absolutely the first sacred text, God's first testament. I recall doing a solo hike in the White Mountains one morning and coming around a corner to be greeted by a family of partridges, a hen and five chicks. We all stopped and stood silently watching each

other for a good amount of time until the birds scampered off under the scrub pines. Then, there was the time I saw a large bird that had been hit and stunned by the car a good distance in front of me. It was on the side of a road, somewhat dazed and unable to fly. I pulled over and approached the bird (some form of raptor like an osprey or eagle) talking very softly. Taking off my jacket, I knelt down and wrapped it around the bird's wings and was about to take it away from the highway into the woods. For a moment, we made eye contact, and I felt a rush of trust, he, having no choice but to trust me and I not even thinking of the potential his beak and talons had. I don't even know how long the moment lasted, but it was sacred as anything I have ever experienced.

4. Music and art – Both music and art (throw in dance and all other forms of art as well) have the power to touch us deeply. Staring at the sculpture of Strazza'a Veiled Virgin, a marble sculpture that seems like you can see through the gossamer-like veil, knowing it is made of stone, (Use the QR to the right to see her), or looking at how Rembrandt made light pass through and illuminate a wave at sea in his masterpiece, Christ in the Storm on the Sea of Galilee (sadly stolen from the Gardner Museum in Boston in 1990), or any piece of art, is so captivating an experience of awe that it can deeply and profoundly affect the viewer for life. I had such a transformative moment in grad school. I was part of the Penn State touring choir, and we were able to perform Beethoven's Ninth Symphony with William Steinberg and the Pittsburgh Symphony orchestra at Carnegie Hall in New York. Steinberg never had us rehearse the entire score just bits and pieces that he wanted to make certain we did right. The night of the performance, Steinberg, an elderly man who couldn't have been more than 5'4" tall, climbed up to the podium. We all knew that the Ninth started with just

two violins playing a high D very quietly, and Steinberg had told us how he wanted it to feel like the dawn of creation. But witnessing this maestro in action was beyond belief! The applause had died off, and Steinberg stood almost motionless staring at the score. It was then that I noticed his right arm, baton in hand, was moving ever so slowly upward. It took forever to get to the top but when he did there was just the slightest flick of his wrist to cue the violins. I think I saw God in that moment. Knowing how the power of the fourth movement we would sing contrasted with the fragility of those first notes was pure awe!

There are other forms of awe that Keltner points to, but you get to read about them on your own! Let me just say that awe is an important aspect of the spiritual journey because of the pivotal role it plays in understanding. Most of us humans are incapable of understanding what and how being spiritual looks like. Stick with me here. I am not insulting your intelligence. I am just saying that there is no right way to get it—there is no road map or formula for reconnecting with your spiritual side. Here's the point: the brain learns by association (the act of comparing new experiences to what it already knows through our past experiences). Our minds need examples it can pattern from. So, when we see someone doing a great humanitarian deed or when behold a place in nature that is beautifully inspiring, our minds think, "Oh, that's what it is!" The mind now has an example or a model it can strive toward, but that example is solely and uniquely yours.

After reading Keltner's book, I was left with the feeling that everything could inspire awe. I refer to it as everyday awe. As we move toward an understanding of spirituality as our way of life, we begin to see the sacred in everything and everyone. There are no longer any ordinary moments when everything is seen as infused with the spirit of love. When I witness children playing, I feel awe. Watching a butterfly emerge from its chrysalis inspires awe. Even noticing how the leaves unfold in the warmth of spring can do it.

An embarrassing example comes to mind as well. At one point we had a massive ant colony on our property—literally, it was 40-50 feet in diameter and probably as deep. We tried everything to get rid of them, including hiring the local pest control professionals, but nothing worked. So, in a fit of frustration—and this is the embarrassing part—I dug about four feet down into the center of the colony and doused the entire thing with a gallon of gasoline. And then I lit it and let it burn! I felt surely that would do the trick. But the next day, I went out to inspect the damage and fell to my knees in awe. The surviving ants were methodically carrying out their dead and burnt comrades and stacking them in a pile off to the side. These were not stupid insects—they were sentient beings! I welled up with tears, being filled with the awe of the moment. In everything, and in everywhere we turn, there are opportunities to see the sacred.

Of course, the common retort to that assertion is, "What about so and so?" or "What about Hitler?" The statement that everything is sacred or everything is a source of awe and spirituality does not mean that we need to accept or condone horrific acts of violence. Rather, it is a stance in life, a way of being from which we choose to operate. Even faced with incivility, hatred, crimes, and violence, we can choose to find the place of spirituality. We can choose to see awe in those who are affected by the violence or find it in some place of refuge that is serving the oppressed. When we look for it, awe is everywhere. But awe is just one source of our spirituality.

The oddity about spirituality is that it is as inseparable from us and our existence as light is from a flame. Spirit is something that either we live or which lives us. Either way, our essence is spirit, thus we are spiritual. When we allow ourselves to be awestruck by these events, not only does that touch our spirit, but the awe of it also triggers bigger and bigger questions. Science has now offered up new and amazing awarenesses that even further boggle our brains. To say that I am spiritual simply means that I feel something stir inside me that brings me in touch with that which is greater than I.

Humans of the past would look up at the starry night sky and wonder what was really out there. Then, at the start of the 17th century, we were gifted with the first telescope, and our eyes widened in greater wonder. Over the next few centuries, the principles of the telescope provided us with ever more powerful telescopes, each revealing more of what we thought was the vastness of our cosmos.

That all changed in 1990 when the Hubble telescope was launched into space. Hubble suddenly revealed stars and galaxies that had never before been seen. Our collective jaws dropped in astonishment at the beauty and detail. But in 2021 Hubble's apparent clarity was blown away by the first images of the James Webb Space Telescope (JWST). JWST was pointed at the dark empty spaces in some parts of the Hubble image areas and revealed millions, perhaps billions, of galaxies where we thought nothing existed.

JWST provided jaw-dropping images! Scientists thought we knew something about the vastness of the universe and suddenly discovered that not only was what we thought less than a fraction of what might be out there but also that we could no longer assume that what we had seen or discovered was anything close to the totality of the universe. Infinity was suddenly relegated to a simple concept that came nowhere close to capturing the reality of the infinite.

On the other end of the scientific spectrum sits the microscope. Microscopes followed a similar path as their telescopic siblings, moving from revealing microbes and protozoa to seeing into the nuclei of cells. Once scanning and transmission electron microscopes were invented, we became aware of elements of the subatomic world. Protons, neutrons, and electrons were not the end of the line in the world of scientific discovery. Atom smashing and other research techniques have revealed elusive sub-entities called bosons, muons and quarks. However, these are extremely difficult to define since they defy most measurement techniques. Yet, the question remains of what may still be found in the spaces in between.

And what of us who are on this spiritual journey? How do we allow our wonder to be charged by each successive scientific discovery? Spiritual mysteries are once again at the core of our wonderment. But old simplistic concepts of God (at least the Michelangelo-type image of God), heaven, and hell (as portrayed by Dante and Botticelli) can no longer hold up in the face of our modern understanding of life, death, and the universe. We are aware that medieval art and literature radically influenced the formation of renaissance theology and realize how very misguided the church was—and continues to be! More important, how do we discover and dissolve the barriers between us and our ability to look at the world with awe and wonder?

The bottom line in discovering, evolving, or rediscovering our spirituality is that it all comes down to knowing that awe-inspiring moments are everywhere and to trusting them. We experience spirituality; we don't think it. Each time you trust the pure experience you have had, you come closer to understanding your own brand of spirituality. Finding Spirit is a matter of allowing yourself to take in and receive the mysterious experience of awe. In a recent blog post on Awakin.org, the late Rabbi Abraham Joshua Heschel describes wonder as "radical amazement," which he considered to be our chief characteristic as spiritual persons. "As civilization advances, the sense of wonder declines. Such decline is an alarming symptom of our state of mind. Mankind will not perish for want of information; but only for want of appreciation. The beginning of our happiness lies in the understanding that life without wonder is not worth living. What we lack is not a will to believe but a will to wonder." The QR to the right will take you to the post (Awakin. org, 2015, https://www.awakin.org/v2/read/view.php?tid=1080).

So, we find ourselves outside and beyond the walls and doctrines of organized religion and into the realm of pure experience. Spirit cannot be known, only experienced. Love cannot be known, only experienced. Wonder cannot be analyzed, only experienced. Where doctrine is all about what can be stated and known, true spirituality can only be experienced. That belongs to you, and no one can say otherwise. I have a Pentecostal friend who still experiences "speaking in tongues." It is not my experience, but it certainly is hers! Another friend of mine is a Buddhist who has taken Boddhisatva vows. He is one of the most spiritual people I know and yet speaks nothing of the Divine or Spirit like I do. Spirit can be found just as easily on a woods walk or on the corner of Times Square in New York City. Spirit shows up when we let it in, no matter who we are, and we are capable of that experience no matter where we are or how we perceive it.

The more we come to know spirituality, the more we understand how little our experience has actually shown us. The universe and the Divine seem so vast that we are incapable of fully grasping it. Yet, at the same time we are humbly aware that what we do know is so little and that little has been revealed to us. Anything we can "know" pales in comparison to the ineffable and incomprehensible. The overwhelming realization at this point is that our experiences are just little glimpses of whatever is at their source. We know without knowing while understanding that we ultimately have no clue of what it is we claim to know. Having dropped all questions and need for answers, we are finally content with not knowing.

Spiritual Health

Identifying the source of our spirituality is but a part of our overall spiritual health. Spiritual health is an integrated process where we have shed our old skins, we've taken out the trash of our old ways to make space for that which is true for us and serves us. Through the dark nights we have progressively decreased the influence of our egos, our little selves, so that our true, big SELF shines through. In short, spiritual health is living and acting from the true self.

Beyond that, we have found a new self-awareness, one that is not a golden idol crafted by the ego but rather that is found to be an integral part of and with everything else. This new self-awareness no longer takes pride in its difference from all else but sees itself through all else and sees all else as a part of the total experience of oneself. We begin to think like Jesus, "I am in you as you are in me, and we are a part of each other."

Through our spiritual side, we have a world view that all is sacred, including even those who annoy and disturb us. Everything is an opportunity for us to act from our mystical roots, remembering that being mystical means trusting our own experience of things. Beyond mere explorers, we have become normal everyday mystics. Our spiritual health provides us with a new set of eyes and ears through which we perceive the world and everything in it. It is all good, including, as I have said, those who annoy or repulse us the most. Through them, we get a window into our shadow selves and those parts of our inner being that we want to reject.[13] Seeing them as me only shows me where I get to do further work. We no longer get to hide behind the pretense of vilifying "them" and own our inner journey and the work ahead.

Spiritual health is not a destination; it is a way of being, and a process through which we live into each new now. It is a way of seeing with an almost childlike awe and wonder and at the same time a way of seeing how we are a part of something far bigger than ourselves. We are able to find the mystical experience in both commonplace as well as those magnificent experiences that would bring us to our knees. Science, nature, people, the universe, and the Divine are all part of this beautiful path of spirituality. We embrace it and rejoice in it.

Spiritual health results in and from our sense of purpose. When we see our place in the vastness of all else, our purpose for being a part of it begins to take shape. We see how the transcendent experiences open us to that greater reality and allow us to see our part. We have a role to play in the grand scheme of things. However, this is nothing like the "God has a plan" mentality of

---

13. Carl Jung's concept of the Shadow Self provides a great insight to the fullness of the SELF and explains it in a way that helps unembraced and work with the shadow instead of denying it.

our more fundamental times. Because we have come to see the divinity in ourselves, within others and all of nature, we are able to take our place in partnership with the creative love as co-authors of our purpose and our future.

Co-Authorship with the Divine

In my book *Typhoon Honey* (Girrell & Sjogren, 2021), we outline the path to becoming the sole and uncontested author of your life. Human transformation is a matter of getting to the substrate level of our beliefs that we hold as truths and either questioning them or rewiring new beliefs in their place, thus changing the trajectory of our lived experience. Spiritual transformation is no different as I have written in my book, *Wrestling the Angel: The Role of the Dark Night of the Soul in Spiritual Transformation* (Girrell, 2015). And while it is true that through the transformational process you can envision and create such an experience, I believe that as created products of this divine experience we call life, we are more like co-authors. When Divine Love exploded in the Big Bang, it infused all forms with the regenerative force of love.[14] Galaxies and star systems are born, die, and recreate themselves as new stars and systems just as we humans are born and can re-create the life in our progeny—though admittedly on a far smaller and less cosmically grand scale!

Therefore, it is no stretch of the imagination to extend that creative process to the path and future of your life. You are imbued with that same creative power of life. The only trick is that you must fully know that you have the power to alter your course by altering your belief systems. When you went through the dark night that is fundamentally what happened! But it is so very easy to slip back into our old habits (read that as ego-driven habits). Your ego wants things the way they have been when it was in control. Nonetheless, you, as part of the Divine creative process, have decided differently. That is where your co-authorship begins. This is neither egotistic nor megalomaniacal. We

---

14. Though this is my personal belief, it is similarly reflected in Ilia Delio's book *Christ in Evolution*. Maryknoll, NY: Orbis Books, 2008.

are not claiming to be God. Rather, we are aware of and acknowledging the presence of a Divine Spirit living within all living things. Spirit is inseparable from us or our soul, just as if you pour a glass of water into the ocean, you will never be able to see what was once the water from the glass because it has become one with the ocean. Co-authorship is simply recognizing that truth.

Journaling. Identify one of the many ways in which you experience awe, and see how many ways you can apply that perception to the other places in your life. Notice that if nature is what inspires you, then how do you embrace the nature—or natural state—in another person. Now, go the next step and apply that same process to that which you find to be ugly, or unworthy of awe. Is a trash heap a place that spawns new life? Does that smelly, old man sitting alone on a park bench still have an innocent child inside? See how many ways you can apply your tools of awe and wonder to things you might not normally consider and write about what comes up. All these examples are part of the platform you create for launching your co-authored life.

CHAPTER FOURTEEN

Belonging is being accepted for you. Fitting in is being accepted for being like everyone else.

Brené Brown

Finding Home

As participation and affiliation with traditional religions decline, we have simultaneously witnessed a sharp increase in isolation and loneliness. While these two dynamics are independently observed, I cannot help but reflect on their relatedness. Obviously, there are many contributing factors to the epidemic of loneliness—the dissolution of nuclear family structure, the prevalence of hand-held devices and various forms of so-called "social media," and a huge societal pressure toward independence—but I am equally certain that the loss of the central role religions and places of worship played as forms of communal connection are significant factors as well.

Explorers on this spiritual journey, people who value and cherish their spirituality, have had to make the difficult choice to forge out on their own, often leaving behind not only their former communities of worship but also, many times, their friends and family of origin. In a way, we who are on this path suffer from spiritual aloneness and spiritual isolation. We long for family and community, and we need to address that yearning head on, lest our longing become so powerful that it forces us back to whence we came!

As we gather our belongings (not those physical things like the special gems, books, and stuff we have collected along the path, but the principles and ideals to which we are aligned), we realize how very few are life-defining. We say things like, "I am not this or that place, I am not defined by where I am or with whom I worship." So, what then shall be our safe harbor in which we anchor? Many of us have searched far and wide, perhaps travelling to India to live in an ashram, camped out in places called vortices of nature, gone to mountain tops, or sat, cross-legged while watching the waves come and go at the ocean's shore. It seems often that no matter where we look, somehow, we find spiritual experiences and are filled with awe. Like those subatomic particles that defy measurement, Spirit morphs to become whatever measure or lens we are using. If we look at the smallest things, it is there. If we contemplate the universe and stare into the images sent by the JWST, it is there. And suddenly (or not so suddenly in my case), we slap our palm to our forehead in awareness.

For many of us, this may come as a surprise realization that wherever we are or with whomever we are in relationship, we, too, are there. Whatever we are viewing, we are the ones perceiving it. We are always just where and only where we are at that moment. The lightning bolt of that realization shoots through us with full power. Home is no longer a place, a safe harbor, or a people with whom we cavort, celebrate, or silently sit with in meditation. Spirit is not something to be sought out there. Home is inside—in this thing we may have once viewed as a skin bag filled with bones, organs, and blood. Home is this temple of and within ourselves, the very place and only place where Spirit ever lives.

We have experienced the sacred and felt the Spirit with our bodies. We have come to think of the Spirit or the Divine not as something "out there" but as in-dwelling and "in here." We think of incarnation not as some historical event that happened to one person or a small handful of ascended masters long ago but as the life within our being. Our beating hearts and breathing lungs are witnesses to the fact that life and the universal love of creation is continually and undeniably within ourselves, this incarnation we call self. I carry my home with me, within me! It is not a burden of heaviness I carry inside my backpack but a lightness of being. This is not the lightness of being Milan Kundera wrote about in his classic book *The Unbearable Lightness of Being* (Kundra, 1984) that I had read some ten or more years ago. Kundera described that lightness as a result of living a moral-less life lacking responsibility. For the main character, there was nothing grounding him.

Rather, this lightness of being that many of us on the path of unitive consciousness now experience is one of freedom from the deadly assumptions with which our toxic religions had loaded us down. Our burdens of guilt and shame have been lifted by the compassion we found for ourselves within ourselves. We have found that there is no longer any "should." Having found divine love and compassion within, living through us, we feel whole and wholly human. We might even say that we feel holy. We have been searching for our home and found it right here, right where we are, right now. It's a feeling that the poet Derek Walcott expresses so well in his poem "Love after Love." He describes the wonderful "reunion" with yourself when you finally discover that home is *where* you are.

In her magnificent book, *Braving the Wilderness* (2017), Dr. Brené Brown describes the feeling of finding home. Drawing inspiration from Saint Maya Angelou, she says that braving the wilderness is a process of getting comfortable within yourself. Quoting Angelou, she writes "You are only free when you realize you belong no place you belong every place and no place at all" (p. 162). Once I discovered that my needing to belong some place anchored my identity and my spirituality to that place, I was able to let go of "place-ness." When no one place was the one to which I belonged, I could actually hang my hat anywhere I was and call it home. Home was no longer a place out there but rather a belonging to myself, right here and right here could be anywhere on the planet. Although Dr. Brown is talking about belongingness as a concept, the same could be said of our spirituality.

> Stop walking through the world looking for confirmation that you don't belong. You will always find it because you've made that your mission. Stop scouring people's faces for evidence that you're not enough. You will always find it because you've made that your goal. True belonging and self-worth are not goods; we don't negotiate their value with the world. The truth about who we are lives in our hearts. Our call to courage is to protect our wild heart against constant evaluation, especially our own. No one belongs here more than you (Brown, 2017, p. 158).

To paraphrase the above, I would say, stop walking through the world looking for where your spirituality doesn't match. Of course, it doesn't match; it's yours. Stop looking for confirmation that your spirituality makes sense to others; it most likely won't because it is yours, alone. True spirituality is not a commodity to be bartered and bargained with. The truth about your spirituality lives within your own heart and soul.

Finding and Creating Home

Finding home is a matter of realizing that spirituality is never an intellectual pursuit. Neither is it about locating the *right place*—a particular church, tradition, or sacred space that suddenly feels like home. Many seekers have spent years searching for the right belief system, the right community, or even the right feeling only to find that their home is not a destination but a way of being.

When we think of home, we realize it is not a single entity but a constellation of relationships—between ourselves, our environment, the Divine (however we name it), and the companions who walk with us. Each of these elements contributes to our sense of spiritual belonging:

You: Home begins within. The more you come to rest in yourself, in your own unfolding journey, the more home becomes something you carry rather than something you must find. It is not about being finished, whole, or certain—it is about being at peace with not knowing, trusting the sacred process of becoming. Coming to grips with yourself as the vehicle of your quest, results in knowing that you carry home with you—within you—no matter where you travel. Home does not exist without you. Like the turtle carries its home with it, you are your own home base. "Wherever you go, there you are" is a saying attributed to numerous pundits. Most of the time it has been used to debunk the "geographic cure," like telling an alcoholic that even if he moves to another state, he will carry his dysfunction with him there. But in our case, we are talking more about our deeper sense of self-awareness. Having shed our egoic false self, we now have a better sense of self and are secure in that SELF.

Place (Time & Space): Home is shaped by where we are in our journey— geographically, emotionally, and spiritually. Sometimes, a physical space nurtures our sense of belonging, whether it is a quiet room, a vast landscape, or a sacred gathering place. Other times, home is found in moments rather than locations: a sunrise, a deep breath, the presence of stillness. When we realize how arbitrary those distinctions are, we suddenly realize that any place and any time can be the defining characteristics of home.

Catch yourself in the spiritual experience, and then sit down, right where you are. It does not matter if you are on Madison Avenue in New York City or some farmland pasture. Notice the moment, and find a place to be still with it—to sit with it. Observe everything about the space and time you are inhabiting at the moment. Say nothing, and in fact, try your best to think nothing, but rather to just observe. Notice the sounds or the stillness. Notice the people if there are any around you. Observe their faces, their pace, where they seem to be headed. Notice the light, the sun or artificial lights that illuminate this sacred moment. Just be still and notice. This, too, is home.

Spirit/God/Universe: Our connection to something greater than ourselves is often what makes us feel at home in the world. But this connection is not something we can chase down, capture, or define on our own terms. The more we try to fit the Divine into our expectations—into a doctrine, an image, a single experience—the more elusive it becomes. Perhaps this is because the sacred is not meant to be grasped but *surrendered to*. Instead of searching for a God that meets our conditions, we may need to let ourselves be *found*—by love, by mystery, by the quiet assurance that we are held, even when we feel lost.

Surrender: Many people dislike the sound of that word, surrender. To them it sounds like giving up—raising the white flag and turning ourselves in. But in the quest of spirituality, surrender is an action taken to receive the spirit. I drop my defenses, and my shields that keep other things out. I let go of the tight grip I hold on how things ought to be. Surrender can be an unfolding. Have you ever crumpled up a piece of cellophane into a ball, then opened your fist to let it expand and unfold back to its original shape? Surrender is the act of letting it unfold and be what it is. It is giving up our strangle hold on life.

We have all had moments where the presence of the Divine seems absent, where silence fills the spaces where certainty once resided. And yet, if we listen carefully, we may begin to recognize that the Spirit within us—the in-dwelling presence that has always been there—has not left us. Like the air we breathe, it does not demand our constant attention to sustain us; it simply *is*. Our spiritual home base is not in a distant heaven, nor is it dependent on external validation. It is in this in-dwelling spirit, the sacred breath that animates us, the love that moves through us whether we acknowledge it or not. In this sense, we are never without home because we carry it within us.

At the same time, our awareness of the totally unfathomable nature of Universal Love—God, Spirit, Source, or whatever name we use for convenience—reminds us that there is nowhere it is *not*. This love does not occupy only the places we designate as holy. It is not confined to temples, churches, or mountaintops. It is as present in the spaces of grief as it is in the moments of ecstasy, as close in the mundane as in the miraculous.

No matter how far we may travel—across lands, across spiritual traditions, across the vastness of our own inner landscapes—the Divine does not remain behind, waiting for our return. It is already where we are going. It was already where we started. There is no place too far, no exile too distant, no wilderness too vast to be beyond the reach of this ever-present Love. The cosmos itself, stretching infinitely beyond our comprehension, is not empty; it is inhabited by the same Divine Spirit that dwells within us.

To be spiritually homeless, then, is not to be abandoned or adrift—it is to be invited into a different kind of belonging. A belonging that is not tied to place, structure, or certainty, but to the living presence of Love itself. Wherever you stand, wherever you wander, you are already wrapped in and enveloped by that Love. You are, and have always been, at home.

Community (Sangha, Fellow Travelers): No one finds home alone. Even the most solitary seekers are shaped by relationships—mentors, soul friends, those who reflect back to them the truth of who they are. Sometimes, these relationships emerge from expected places: a wise teacher, a sacred text, or a faith tradition that offers guidance. But often, they come in surprising forms—a stranger on the same journey, an author whose words resonate across time, or a fleeting conversation that lingers in the heart long after it has ended.

Community does not always look like a congregation, nor does belonging always require a formal group membership. For some, the old structures of religious affiliation no longer provide a sense of home, but this does not mean they must walk alone. Home can be found in the quiet companionship of a friend who listens without judgment, in the unspoken understanding between those who have wrestled with similar doubts, in the shared silence of those who are learning to embrace mystery together. Sometimes, home is simply knowing that others are searching, too.

My wife and I were in Istanbul recently and having breakfast at the BandB, where we were staying a few days. Sitting by himself near the window was an interesting-looking man, so I invited myself to join him for breakfast. The conversation that followed was nothing short of amazing. His name was Basil Savitsky; he described himself as a semi-retired professor, author, philosopher, futurist, and strategic consultant! Our interests, philosophies, and the people whose writings we each devoured were similar. We could have talked for hours were it not that we each had tours scheduled or a boat to catch. So, we decided to meet for breakfast the next day as well. He, like me, is a spiritual seeker.

We commented that when you are a seeker, you see other seekers so easily; you find homes everywhere you look. We exchanged business cards since it was our last day in Istanbul, and I thought nothing more of him until a day ago when I received an email from him with the preface to his newest book. But the point I want to make here is that these things are not chance happenings or miracles of some sort. They are the way this journey looks.

There is an old proverb from the time of Confucius that says, *"Two thieves who meet on the road don't need an introduction."* The same is true for seekers, mystics, wanderers—those who are learning to navigate the liminal space of spiritual homelessness. When we encounter another who has walked a similar path, no formal introduction is needed. There is a knowing, a silent recognition that speaks louder than words.

Michael Adam Beck is a United Methodist minister, college professor, author and thought-leader whose passion is creating communities of spirituality in non-church-like settings. He conducts gatherings in restaurants for "dinner church," in public parks, and even a tattoo parlor. Leading the UMC emerging practice called Fresh Expressions, Beck and his

friends and colleagues have been providing spaces for spiritual expression for others on this journey of the Spiritual but not Religious and have been teaching others—which he calls planting seeds—how to grow communities outside the traditions and structures of formal religion. Michel proves that there are many other places and communities within which we can meet our siblings on this path of discovery. The QR to the right will take you to his webpage with links to his many books and current writings in his Substack.

For those who feel spiritually homeless, the invitation is not to search harder but to shift perspective. Instead of striving to find a place where everything finally makes sense, perhaps home is where we allow ourselves to *rest in the questions.* Perhaps it is not about clinging to certainty but about standing in the openness of unknowing, trusting that something sacred is present even in the uncertainty. Instead of longing for a structure that perfectly fits, perhaps home is found in the spaces where we are free to grow—where we are not required to conform but instead encouraged to expand.

Some 15 years ago, I happened onto the campus of Rolling Ridge Retreat and Conference Center in North Andover, Massachusetts. Though it isn't very far from my house, I had never heard of it in the 30 years I lived in this area. Rolling Ridge is a beautiful 1920's award-winning property that is a haven of peace and quiet. There I found walking labyrinths, benches overlooking the lake, and inside the building, I found friendship and fellow seekers. Eventually after many return trips, I have become a member of their Board of Directors. In a way I found a piece of home, one which I am dedicated to preserving for other seekers like me.

Home, then, is not necessarily a destination or a return to something familiar. It is the place where we stop striving to *arrive* and instead begin to recognize that we are already held, already connected, already enough. It is the realization that we belong not because we have found the perfect faith, the perfect people, or the perfect place, but because we are part of something larger than ourselves—something vast, unfolding, and always welcoming us deeper into the mystery of being.

In terms of the Divine, we have found that the in-dwelling Spirit is always with us—even when we do not perceive it. It is the quiet presence that remains when certainty fades, the gentle hum beneath our thoughts, the unshakable current of love that carries us even when we feel lost. It is what makes you and me divine in our own right. Whether we call it God, Spirit, Universal Love, or something else entirely, this sacred presence does not depend on our awareness of it. It does not vanish when we doubt, nor does it withdraw when we wander. If anything, it is in our wandering that we often come to realize it was never absent. It was not absent because it is our own essence—our own divinity.

This in-dwelling Spirit is our true spiritual home base—not a place we must strive to reach but something we already carry within us. It is not confined to a building, a doctrine, or a sacred text but is woven into the very fabric of our being. In this sense, we are never truly homeless; we are always at home with Spirit because Spirit is always at home in us. No matter how restless our seeking, no matter how many identities we shed, or how many spiritual landscapes we traverse, this inner dwelling remains—steady, unshaken, quietly holding us.

And yet, paradoxically, if we are at home with the Spirit within, we are also at home everywhere because there is nowhere Spirit is not. The totally unfathomable nature of Divine Love means that it is not bound by borders or by human constructs of space and time. It is present in the vast stillness of a cathedral and in the chaotic beauty of a bustling street. It is in the places where we feel awe and in the places where we feel abandoned. It is in the depth of space, in the pulse of a star billions of light-years away, just as much as it is in the smallest, most hidden corners of our everyday lives.

No matter how far we travel—whether across countries, through spiritual traditions, or even into the cosmos itself—the Divine is already there, waiting for us to recognize what was never absent. The invitation is not to search for Love as if it were lost but to awaken to the reality that we are already wrapped in it, enveloped by it, inseparable from it. To be spiritually homeless, then, is not about lacking a place to belong, but about learning to see that *everywhere* is sacred and that we ourselves are always at home in Love.

But where do you find *your people*, your community of fellow travelers? The answer is both simpler and more profound than we often assume. It is not merely a matter of looking in the places you frequent—though sometimes, familiarity can hold unexpected treasures. Nor is it a quest for something hidden in sacred sites, mystical gatherings, or the pilgrimage destinations we often associate with enlightenment. While those places may indeed bring us into contact with others on a similar path, the true encounter—the recognition of kindred spirits—happens not in the searching, but in the *seeing*.

When we are actively seeking confirmation, scanning every interaction for signs that we have found "our people," we are often driven by ego's neediness— the longing to belong, to be affirmed, to be reassured that we are not alone. But belonging is not something to be *grasped*; it is something to be *recognized*. And recognition comes only when we release the striving, when we no longer demand that community look a certain way, speak a certain language, or meet a predetermined set of expectations.

It is a paradox of spiritual seeking that the moment we stop desperately looking for fellow travelers, with the assumption that we must be the only ones like this, we begin to notice that they have been there all along. Once we surrender the need for certainty, once we open the eyes of our heart, we start to see the connections that were always present. We find them in the person sitting next to us on the train, in a conversation with a stranger over a guest house breakfast, in a shared moment of quiet understanding. We begin to recognize that spiritual kinship is less about common belief and more about common resonance—the deep hum of something familiar in another's soul.

So, the question is not *where* to find your people but *how* to recognize them. The answer is deceptively simple: Be present. Be open. Let go of expectations, and trust that those who are meant to walk alongside you will appear—not because you went searching but because you were willing to see.

I see you! You are not alone. In fact, there are thousands upon thousands of us in America and even more around the world. You will know each other by the light you see reflected in their eyes, their way of being, and their remarkable presence. You are like that. You are the face of the new world of spirituality. Spirituality is and always has been an experience, however fleeting, that was available only in the present moment and you are always in the moment of now if you choose to be.

Journaling. If home is always where you are in the moment, how would you describe your place of living or thriving? What would your "home" be like? If you were to create a sanctuary where you could be at home within yourself there, what would it look like? Where would it be? Write a description of your idealized sacred workshop, putting in as much detail as you can.

CHAPTER FIFTEEN

Practice what you know, and it will help to
make clear what now you do not know.

Rembrandt

So what – Now what?

There are three questions I live with on a daily basis: **What's so? So what? And now what?** These three questions serve as a kind of spiritual compass, guiding me through the uncertainty of faith, belonging, and meaning. They are not meant to provide definitive answers but to open the door to deeper engagement with the mystery of existence.

What's So? – Interrogating Reality

The first question—**What's so?**—is about exposing the truth of what is really happening, not what I *think* is happening. I often call this practice **interrogating reality** because it requires an intentional stripping away of assumptions, biases, and conditioned perceptions (Scott, 2004).

At a basic level, we know that our senses deceive us. Our eyes do not actually "see" reality as it is. Instead, they act as receptors, feeding fragmented bits of data to the brain, which then translates those signals into recognizable images. The brain does not interpret these data points neutrally—it filters them through memory, past experience, cultural conditioning, and deeply ingrained narratives. What I perceive is not the raw truth of the world but a story I have unconsciously constructed about it.

A while back, I decided to run a marathon. My endomorphic body type is not one you would normally see running long distances. Those guys and gals are lean and fit. I, on the other hand, have always been probably 20 pounds above those charts doctors always refer to. In any case, after a year of heavy training I actually had shed those 20 extra pounds and then some. One morning shortly before Marathon Day, I woke up and was shocked. Instead of the semi-chubby body I was used to seeing, I had somehow woken up in an athlete's body. My stomach was flat and firm, and I could see the lines between my abs. My legs were muscular and well defined. In my half-awake state, the image sent to my groggy brain was not of my body. But by the time I got to the bathroom, my brain was awake enough to translate the image and what I saw in the mirror was the body I was used to. Try as I may, I could not see the fit and trim athlete whose strange body I woke up in—my mind could not tolerate the dissonance so it changed the information it was receiving through my rods and cones to match what it "knew" to be true!

To interrogate reality is to pause and ask: *Is this real? What do you see, or is this simply what you have been trained to see?* It takes practice—daily, moment-by-moment practice—to ground oneself in presence and to peel back the layers of interpretation. Some call this mindfulness; others call it contemplation. It is the art of noticing without immediately assigning meaning, of suspending the compulsion to categorize, explain, or control. And it is this practice—learning to see without illusion—that begins to dissolve the barriers between what we think we know and the deeper, more ungraspable truth beneath it.

Key questions for the **What's So** phase: What happened? What did you observe? What issue is being addressed (or what population is being served)? What were the results of the project? What events or "critical incidents" occurred? How can I trust or corroborate what I am seeing? What was of particular notice? How did I feel about that?

In the pain of our spiritual crises and dark nights, we saw only our separateness: separate from anything Divine, separate from others, even our friends and families, and separate even from ourselves. In this dissociative state we incorrectly concluded that we were alone, but after interrogating reality, we found instead that all of that was an illusion. It wasn't that we were alone but rather that we had created this false sense of separateness.

So What? - Making Meaning

The second question—**So what?**—forces me to consider the significance of what I have seen. It is one thing to observe reality; it is another to discern *why it matters*. This question keeps me from drifting into spiritual nihilism, where everything is just a series of events without deeper significance.

This is where things get complicated—because meaning is not something inherent in events; it is something we *assign* to them. And when we find ourselves spiritually homeless, untethered from the meaning systems we once relied upon, it can feel as though we are left adrift in a world where nothing holds weight.

But perhaps that is the invitation: *To become active participants in the unfolding of meaning rather than passive recipients of inherited belief systems.* If home is not a fixed location, if God is not a being that exists within definable borders, then meaning, too, must be something fluid—something created and recreated in relationship with the world around us.

Asking **So what?** invites us to explore meaning not as an absolute, but as something organic. It allows us to hold paradox—to accept that some moments are sacred without knowing why, that suffering can transform without needing to be justified, that love can exist without needing a name.

Key questions for the **So What** phase: Did you learn a new skill or clarify an interest? Did you hear, smell, feel anything that surprised you? What feelings or thoughts seem most strong today? How is your experience different from what you expected? What struck you about that? How was that significant? What impacts the way you view the situation/experience? (What is the lens through which you are viewing?) What do these critical incidents mean to you? How did you want to respond to them? What did you like/dislike about the experience and why are you judging them that way?

Asking **So what?** transforms that illusion of separateness we discovered in the previous questioning of what's so. The answer is that, if we have made up the perception of aloneness that our ego had thrown up as our obstacle, then we are free and capable of creating a new interpretation. It substantially alters our base of operation from one of looking for confirmation that we are alone to that of seeking confirmation that we are never alone. And, as we know, the mind will always find evidence to support its operating assumptions. You are the maker of meaning—use that skill to serve you, your quest, and your higher purpose.

Now What? – Living Into the Mystery

The final question, **Now what?** is about action. It asks: *How do I move forward in light of what I now see? What does it mean to live in response to what has been revealed?*

For those of us who feel spiritually homeless, this question is not about returning to our former home, or to the old maps, nor is it about rushing to construct a new one. Instead, it is an invitation to *walk without a map*, to step forward without demanding certainty. It asks us to trust the unfolding—to believe that even without rigid doctrines or defined structures, love is still at work in the world, and we are still part of that movement. One of my teachers, Judith Rich, walks along the beach of the bay every morning, greeting the (mostly) homeless people who she sees there. But her context is that these are just "friends I haven't met yet." She looks for the friendship that she assumes is already there – and she finds it every time. In a very similar way, when we walk this path assuming we are never alone, we find friends everywhere, we find the sacred everywhere and we find our spirit thriving in each encounter and each moment. Asking now what is an open invitation to step into what is next. We are really asking what the next right thing to do is, without knowing or seeing an end point.

Key questions to be answered in the **Now What** phase: What seems to be the root causes of the issue/problem addressed? What kinds of activities are currently taking place in the community related to this project or issue? What contributes to the success of projects like this? What hinders success? What learning occurred for you in this experience? How can you apply this learning? What would you like to learn more about related to this project or issue? What follow-up is needed to address any challenges or difficulties? What information can you share with your peers or community volunteers? If you were in charge of the project, what would you do to improve it? If you could do the project again, what would you do differently? What would "complete" the picture?

The spiritual path is not about *having* the answers, but about learning to *live* the questions, **What's so? So what? Now what?** These questions do not resolve the ache of spiritual homelessness, but they transform it. They shift our focus from searching for a fixed place of belonging to discovering that home is something we *practice*—with each act of awareness, with each moment of meaning-making, with each step we take into the unknown.

And in that movement, in that trust, we again find that we were never truly lost at all. We find instead that "it" was there all along but that we had looking with the wrong set of eyes. When we look through the eyes of love and compassion, all we ever see is opportunity after opportunity to live that love and compassion.

What I have written on these pages has been my best effort in describing what's so for those of us on this spiritual journey. I have written about the journey of the spiritual seeker, while being on that journey *as* a seeker, myself. I have used the words of others and my own best approximation of reality as I have experienced it. Be that as it may, we need to continually recycle through the questions of what's so, so what, and now what.

Each of you has taken your own meaning of what's so for you and ask your own kind of "so what" questions. What are we to make of all of this? What are we to do as a result of having struggled through this wilderness? It is a powerful question. What do you make of it? What does it all mean to you?

I will not pretend to answer those questions for you but can only answer my own "so what?" And there are several responses that come up for me. The first and perhaps most preemptive is how might I continue this journey? What are the tools and disciplines that have worked thus far and that might sustain me on my journey through the next iterations? What I have come up with are two key practices.

Practicing Presence

First, I need to learn how to stay present to each experience as it occurs. I know now that my brain will want to classify and label each experience and that as soon as I do that I am no longer in the experience. So, the trick for me and the discipline I must practice is to learn how to stay in the experience without labeling it. I must actively fight the urge to say, "this is that." I know that takes practice—a lot of practice because it is my mind's job to do what it does and doing that takes me immediately out of the experience. Here are some favorite suggestions for practicing presence:

- Breathe

- Feel your feet on the ground

- Immerse yourself in nature

- Take a walk and speak the colors or textures you see

- Ritually wash your face or hands, or take a hot bath/shower

- Drink a cup of hot tea and name the flavors you taste

- Play a song and move your body to it the way it is longing to move

- Write through it – journalling is your friend

- Embodied spiritual practice

- Lay flat on the earth spread-eagle

- Reach out to a friend, spiritual mentor, or therapeutic practitioner

- Continue doing the practice that you know works for you!

Practicing Non-judgment

The practice I am learning is non-judgment. It goes like this: Try to not label anything as good or bad or something you like or dislike for the next hour. Just one hour! We are so accustomed to popping a "thumbs up" icon on Instagram or Facebook that it has become second nature. But life doesn't need us to swipe right or left to the experience it presents. We need to learn how to stay in it without having an opinion *about* it. And that is hard, really hard to do. So, try it out. Just for an hour. And if you get there, then try for two or for a half day. Over time, you can learn to see things as they are—just for what they are.

Try doing that with yourself. Who are you without your assessment of who you are? Who are you without your evaluative judgments of liking this part and not liking that part? Most of us can't even look at our bodies without judgements. We like our smile and hate our pudgy stomachs. Our teeth are crooked (unless some orthodontist fixed them early on), our weight is not ideal, our genitalia are too small or too big or just plain ugly. Worse yet (see the judgment there?) we may have an evaluation or a dislike of our aging bodies—believe me at 76, I find myself copping an attitude about this formerly athletic body of mine! We have opinions about every part of us. But when we are able to let go of all of those judgments, we are left with the simple statement of "I am what I am." Isn't that, as we have learned, the holiest of all statements? "I am."

If we can begin to practice being judgment free with ourselves we may have a shot at being judgment free of others and of other parts of our experience. Don't get me wrong! I am nowhere near mastery of this skill, but I do practice it and try my best to learn how to do it with some regularity. Losing our need for evaluation and judgment is part of a larger practice of presencing or staying present to the experience we are having to the reality as it actually is.

And now it is time to say farewell. I want to thank you for joining me on this trek, but I know that we are all on our own unique paths and that those paths inevitably diverge. So, for now perhaps we part ways, knowing that we will no doubt cross paths again somewhere and some time. And for now, we part ways in the deeply held knowledge that we are never alone. Through our collective spirituality, we are forever entangled with each other.

It may be obvious by now, but one of my spiritual practices is reading poetry—something I highly recommend! I will leave you with one last poem from a writer who understands the process of being shaped by forces greater than ourselves, who surrenders to life as a growth process.

I want to age like sea glass
- By Bernadette Noll -

I want to age like sea glass.
Smoothed by tides, not broken.
I want the currents of life to toss me around,
shake me up and leave me feeling washed clean.

I want my hard edges to soften as the years pass
made not weak but supple.
I want to ride the waves, go with the flow,
feel the impact of the surging tides rolling in and out.
When I am thrown against the shore
and caught between the rocks and a hard place,
I want to rest there until I can find the strength to do what is next.
Not stuck just waiting, pondering,
feeling what it feels like to pause.
And when I am ready,
I will catch a wave and let it carry me along
to the next place that I am supposed to be.
I want to be picked up on occasion by an unsuspected soul
and carried along—just for the connection,
just for the sake of appreciation and wonder.
And with each encounter,
new possibilities of collaboration are presented,
and new ideas are born.
I want to age like sea glass
so that when people see the old woman I'll become,
they'll embrace all that I am.
They'll marvel at my exquisite nature,
hold me gently in their hands and be awed by my well-earned patina.
Neither flashy nor dull, just a perfect luster.
And they'll wonder, if just for a second,
what it is exactly I am made of and how I got to this very here and now.
And we'll both feel lucky to be in that perfectly right place
at that profoundly right time.
I want to age like sea glass.
I want to enjoy the journey and let my preciousness be,
not in spite of the impacts of life, but because of them.

Many blessings to you, until we meet again.

Kris

Bibliography and Works Cited

Barks, C. (2001). *The essential Rumi*. HarperCollins. (Original work published 1995).

Benefiel, M. (2008). *The soul of a leader: Finding your path to success and fulfillment*. Crossroad Publishing Co.

Benner, D. (2011). *Soulful spirituality: Becoming fully alive and deeply human*. Brazos Press.

Bessey, S. (2024). *Fieldnotes from the wilderness: Practices for an evolving faith*. Convergent Books.

Bidwell, D. (2018). *When one religion isn't enough: The lives of spiritually fluid people*. Beacon Press.

Bondi, R. (1987). *To love as God loves: Conversations with the early church*. Fortress Press.

Bragdon, E. (2013). *The call of spiritual emergency: From personal crisis to personal transformation*. Harper & Row.

Brown, B. (2017). *Braving the wilderness: The quest for true belonging and the courage to stand alone*. Random House.

Buckley, M. J. (1979). *Atheism and contemplation* [Unpublished paper]. Jesuit School of Theology, Berkeley. https://theologicalstudies.net/articles/ateism-and-contemplation/.

Campbell, J. (2001). *Thou art that: Transforming religious metaphor.* New World Library.

Coleman, G. and Jinpa T. (2005). The Tibetan book of the dead. Penguin Books.

Cummings, e. e. (1958) *All which isn't singing is mere talking.* AllPoetry. https://allpoetry.com/all-which-isn't-singing-is-mere-talking

Deida, D. (2005). *Finding God through sex: Awakening the one of spirit through the two of flesh.* Sounds True.

Davis, J., Graham, M., & Burge, R. P. (2023). *The great dechurching: Who's leaving, Why are they going, and What will bring them back?* (pp. 4–5). Zondervan Reflective.

Delio, I. (2008). *Christ in evolution.* Orbis Books.

Ehrman, B. (2015). *How Jesus became God: The exaltation of a Jewish preacher from Galilee.* HarperOne.

FitzGerald, C. (1984). Impasse and dark night. In T. Edwards (Ed.), *Living with apocalypse: Spiritual resources for social compassion* (pp. 93-116). HarperCollins.

Finley, J. (2013, April 18–20). *The Divine ambush* [Lecture presentation]. Center for Action and Contemplation, Santa Fe, NM.

Fowler, J. (1995). *The stages of faith: The psychology of human development and the quest for meaning.* HarperCollins.

Girrell, K. (2017). *Wrestling the angel: The role of the dark night of the soul in spiritual transformation.* CreateSpace Independent Publishing.

Girrell, K., & Sjogren, C. (2021). *Typhoon honey: The only way out is through.* MSI Press.

Grof, S., & Grof, C. (1989). *Spiritual emergency: When personal transformation becomes a crisis.* Jeremy Tarcher/Putnam.

Harris, S. (2015). *Waking up: A guide to spirituality without religion.* Simon & Schuster.

Hathaway, K. B. (2000). *The little locksmith.* The Feminist Press at CUNY.

Holmes, B. A. (2021). *Crisis contemplation: Healing the wounded village.* CAC Publishing.

James, W. (1905/2022). *The varieties of religious experience: Lecture III – The reality of the unseen.* Longmans, Green and Company. (CrossRoads reprint)

St John of the Cross. (2008). *Ascent of Mount Carmel* (A. Peers, Trans.; Original work published 1946). Dover Publications.

St John of the Cross. (2003). *Dark night of the soul* (A. Peers, Trans.; Original work published 1953). Dover Publications.

Johnston, W. (1995). *Mystical theology: The science of love.* Orbis Books.

Loder, J. (1998). *The logic of the spirit: Human development in theological perspective.* Jossey-Bass.

Keltner, D. (2023). *Awe: The new science of everyday wonder and how it can transform your life.* Penguin Press.

Kolodiejchuk, B. (2007). *Mother Teresa: Come be my light.* Doubleday.

Kübler-Ross, E. (1969). *On death and dying.* Scribner.

Kundera, M. (1984) *The unbearable lightness of being.* Harper Perennial

Loder, J. E. (1998). *The logic of the spirit: Human development in theological perspective.* Jossey-Bass.

May, G. (2004). *The dark night of the soul: A psychiatrist explores the connection between darkness and spiritual growth.* HarperCollins.

Oliver, M. (1992). *New and selected poems.* Beacon Press.

Packard, J., & Hope, A. (2015). *Church refugees: Sociologists reveal why people are done with church but not their faith.* Group Publishing.

Palmer, P. (2009) *The clearness committee: A communal approach to discernment.* Courage & Renewal. in Parker J. Palmer, *A hidden wholeness: The journey toward an undivided life.* Jossey-Bass

Peck, M. S. (1978). *The road less traveled: A new psychology of love, traditional values, and spiritual growth.* Simon & Schuster.Rohr, R., & Finley, J. (2012). *Intimacy: The Divine ambush* [Audio recording]. Center for Action and Contemplation. https://cac.org.

Schachter-Shalomi, Z., & Miller, R. S. (1995). *From age-ing to sage-ing: A profound new vision for growing older.* Grand Central Publishing.

Scharmer, C. O. (2007). *Theory U: Leading from the future as it emerges.* SOL (Society for Organizational Learning).

Scott, S. (2004). *Fierce conversations: Achieving success at work and in life, one conversation at a time.* Penguin Group.

Stafford, C., & Stafford, G. (2022). *Walking with the spiritual but not religious: Spiritual companions for a post-religious world.* Apocryphile Press.

Starr, M. (Ed.). (2008). *Saint John of the Cross: Devotions, prayers & living wisdom* (pp. 71–73). Sounds True.

Starr, M. (Ed.). (2022). *Julian of Norwich: The showings.* Hampton Roads Publishing.

Taylor, B. B. (2014). *Learning to walk in the dark*. HarperCollins.

The Cloud of Unknowing (W. Johnston, Trans.). (1996). Image Books. (Original work published ca. 1375).

Tickle, P. (2008). *The great emergence: How Christianity is changing and why*. Baker Books.

Tickle, P. (2012). *Emergence Christianity: What is it, where is it going, and why does it matter*. Baker Books.

Tillich, P. (1948). *The shaking of the foundations*. Scribner.

Underhill, E. (2009). *Mysticism*. Evinity Publishing Inc.

Weems, R. J. (1999). *Listening for God: A minister's journey through silence and doubt*. Touchstone.

Weil, S. (1951). *Waiting for God* (E. Craufurd, Trans.). Harper & Row.

Whyte, D. (1989). *The opening of eyes*. In *Songs for coming home*. Many Rivers Press.

Whyte, D, (2007). *The well of grief*. In *River Flow: New & Selected Poems*. Many Rivers Press.

Wilber, K. (2007). *Integral spirituality: A startling new role for religion in the modern and postmodern world*. Shambhala Press.

Yacoboni, C. (2014). *How do you pray? Inspiring responses from religious leaders, spiritual guides, healers, activists & other lovers of humanity*. Monkfish Book Publishing.

Zelizer, J. (2021). Abraham Joshua Heschel: A life of radical amazement. Yale University Press.

www.ingramcontent.com/pod-product-compliance
Lightning Source LLC
Chambersburg PA
CBHW070602100426
42744CB00006B/379